helping families recover from addiction

Coping, Growing, and Healing through
12-STEP PRACTICES
and *IGNATIAN SPIRITUALITY*

JEAN HEATON

LOYOLA PRESS.
A JESUIT MINISTRY

Chicago

LOYOLA PRESS.
A JESUIT MINISTRY

3441 N. Ashland Avenue
Chicago, Illinois 60657
(800) 621-1008
www.loyolapress.com

Scripture quotations contained herein are from the *New Revised Standard Version Bible: Catholic Edition*, copyright ©1993 and 1989 by the Division of Christian Education of the National Council of the Churches of Christ in the U.S.A. Used by permission. All rights reserved.

The Twelve Steps of Alcoholics Anonymous are adapted with permission of Alcoholics Anonymous World Services, Inc. ("A.A.W.S."). Permission to adapt the Twelve Steps does not mean that A.A.W.S. has reviewed or approved the contents of this publication, or that A.A.W.S. necessarily agrees with the views expressed herein. A.A. is a program of recovery from alcoholism only—use of the Twelve Steps in connection with programs and activities which are patterned after A.A., but which address other problems, or in any other non-A.A. context, does not imply otherwise. *Additionally, while A.A. is a spiritual program, A.A. is not a religious program. Thus, A.A. is not affiliated or allied with any sect, denomination, or specific religious belief.*

The poem "The Guest House" on p. 125 is from *The Essential Rumi* Translations by Coleman Barks. Copyright ©1995 by Coleman Barks. Reprinted by permission. All rights reserved.

Cover art credit: Catherine MacBride/Moment Open/Getty Images

ISBN: 978-0-8294-4926-6
Library of Congress Control Number: 2020943067

Printed in the United States of America.
20 21 22 23 24 25 26 27 28 29 Versa 10 9 8 7 6 5 4 3 2 1

To my family: past, present, and future.

Contents

Introduction

We live in a world where most people still subscribe to the belief that shame is a good tool for keeping people in line. Not only is this wrong, but it's dangerous. Shame is highly correlated with addiction, violence, aggression, depression, eating disorders and bullying. . . . If we can share our story with someone who responds with empathy and understanding, shame can't survive.

—Brené Brown, *Daring Greatly*

One afternoon a couple of years ago, I was reading a book upstairs in our bonus room. It was a cold day, but I had a dog tucked on either side of me keeping me warm. My phone dinged, alerting me to a text message. It was from a young mom I knew from church. She was trying to remember a prior conversation we'd had about the cause of addiction, since she knew my family had experienced it firsthand with my son's addiction.

"There are many theories on the cause," I told her. "More and more, I've read that toxic shame is at the root of all addictions."

"That's it. I remember now," she said.

As we continued to text, there was something about the direction of the conversation that caught my attention. I couldn't really put my finger on it, but it made me feel as if I needed to be on guard.

She asked about the kinds of people who talked to me about my experience and the kinds of things they wanted to know. Her comments and questions seemed to dance around judgment, whether real or imagined. So, I decided to give her what I figured she wanted to hear. No more dancing, I thought. I will just dive right in.

"Most people are just curious about what *I* did wrong," I texted, expecting that she would be as offended by that statement as I was as I typed it.

Rapid-fire, she wrote back, "What did you do wrong? That is something I would be interested in hearing."

For the record, texting conversations can be difficult to read without seeing someone's facial expression or hearing her tone of voice. I guess I got what I deserved, texting glibly and leaving myself open to her response. However, the direct nature of her words both stung and shocked me.

Thankfully, we weren't able to go any further because she got a phone call. I am certain that was God's grace because I needed time to sit with our conversation. More importantly, I needed to unpack my feelings.

I tried to place myself in her shoes. This young mother couldn't understand the stigma that surrounds addiction. She hadn't been on the other side of it. She'd never heard the pejorative language used to describe alcoholics or addicts applied to her child. I knew I felt hurt by the situation, yet I also knew I had been the one to open the door and invite it in. She was unsuspecting of my sarcasm and trusted me, but I had expected the worst of her. I was the one doing the judging.

This is why I can't trust people from church, I thought. My anger began to boil, so I took a deep breath and figured I should pray for her. I did—but for good measure, I asked for a little help for myself, too.

Soon, I felt my heart begin to soften. The anger started to subside as my vision began to clear. Perhaps I heard God laugh as well. Truthfully, the thing that had once felt so devastating—my son's addiction—had become life-changing. I had been itching to share what it had brought into my life, but I hadn't yet pinpointed what I could give to others that would be of value. So, why, when this young woman asked me that question, did it offend me so?

I remembered that a few weeks before, I couldn't wait to watch the Diane Sawyer interview with Dylan Klebold's mother (of the Columbine High School shooting). I wanted to hear what she had to say, not so I could judge or look down on her. No, I wanted to know what not to do, just as this young mother from church wanted to learn from me.

What is it we need to do to keep our kids safe? How can we keep them from making choices that could ruin their lives? I think those are questions to which all parents would like the answers.

During the years of my son's active addiction, I read blogs written by parents who were affected by a child's drinking and/or drug use. These parents carried a lot of regret, shame, and blame on their shoulders. They searched high and low for a way to help their kids battle the disease. They went to doctors, tried rehab after rehab, talked to counselors, attended twelve-step meetings, and basically wore holes in the knees of their pants praying for their loved ones. With addiction, there are so many variables at play. We grasp at straws, trying different things to fix our loved ones.

Perhaps the sting I felt from the woman's question was a reaction to my own questions. Did I do something that had harmed my child so severely that he ran to drugs and alcohol to escape? That question had gnawed at me for some time. I was too afraid to utter it out loud, and now she had directed it towards me with such ease: What did you do wrong?

My twelve-step group taught me that with this disease, we need to remember we didn't *cause* it, we can't *cure* it, and we can't *control* it. In the program, these are referred to as the three C's. But there is a fourth

C. We can *contribute* to it. And *that* is something we *can* change. I still have influence over *my* actions.

So, what did I contribute to my loved one's disease?

In all honesty, a lot. Of course, it was never my intention to hurt my child. But my actions may have been wrong in ways I didn't even know. The good news is that there are things we can do that aid our own recovery. In turn, our loved ones will be affected by our positive changes. We can learn new ways that will contribute to our loved one's recovery instead of the disease.

———

Many years ago, my reaction to the young woman's text would have been very different. Instead of slowing down, looking for the root of my feelings, examining my intentions, and praying my way through the situation, I'm fairly certain I would have blown my top, harbored resentment, and gossiped about her instead.

When I looked at my hurt feelings, though, I was able to trace them back to shame. Like the account of the Fall in Genesis 3, when Adam and Eve were tempted with the fruit that would allow them to know more, I wanted to *be* more. I wanted to be above this disease. I wanted to be different than the people in my family who suffered from this disease. I felt sure that my current family would be the exception.

This need to be more was basically my own personal "fig leaf," covering the fear and shame I had inherited from my father. His father, who died before I was born, was an alcoholic. Accordingly, the fear of alcoholism and addiction was very real to my father. I grew up hearing the cautionary tales of the damage this disease causes. For my dad, the disease caused physical abuse, loss of education, and inability to afford the next meal. He lived in pursuit of becoming more than the place he'd come from.

The truth is, I never thought much about my grandfather until the disease of addiction came to roost at my front door. I never understood my father's pain until I was forced to face our problems head on, as my husband and son, who both suffer from the disease, struggled with recovery.

This is a family disease. I didn't understand that until I began my twelve-step program; nor did I know how much my father and grandfather had affected how I raised my children. Only when addiction had come into my home did I begin to look at myself and my part in the problem.

I've since learned that this disease carries tremendous shame, both for the addicted and for the families who love them. I'd known for some time that something wasn't right with our son, but I was afraid to look too closely at the problem until things began to spiral out of control. Then, as a mother, I felt I must have done something terribly wrong. Shame was one of the primary reasons I stayed hidden—that is, until it became a burden so great that it forced me out of hiding and gave me the courage to ask for help.

In an effort to make sense of our situation, I did what I saw those other parents doing: I blogged about it, read books, went to twelve-step meetings; my husband dealt with his problem with alcohol, and we participated in marriage and family counseling. I explored the spirituality of St. Ignatius and discovered its parallels to my twelve-step program. I sought spiritual direction and attended retreats.

Over time, I began talking to others about our situation. I wanted to share our experience and how we had found strength and hope. But it took a long time to get there. I was afraid to share due to my fear of the judgment others might have about our family. I felt I could not trust the information with just anyone, not even my church family. I had started an anonymous blog, which caught the attention of other bloggers going through the same process. In the safety of that community, I began to open up.

Twelve-step meetings were another sanctuary. The people in those groups were the most accepting, nonjudgmental people I had ever met. Their truthful and open sharing gave me the courage to take off my mask of shame. It was there that I began to get a vision of what unconditional love might look like.

I read in John Bradshaw's book *Healing the Shame That Binds You* that in the account of the Fall in Genesis 3, four relationships were broken by Adam's toxic shame: the relationship between us and God, our relationship with ourselves, our relationship with our fellow brothers and sisters, and our relationship with society. With all of these broken relationships, our lives become disordered. Bradshaw teaches that the Twelve Steps go about restoring that order. As I began to work the Twelve Steps, I was amazed to discover how life-changing they were. They could be applied to any situation. Why didn't everyone know about them?

You see, I had looked for something within the Catholic Church to guide me in our family crisis. I spent hours searching for any book that talked about how Catholics might approach alcoholism and addiction in keeping with the church's teaching. I didn't want to do anything wrong. We were in such a fragile position.

When I looked up the history of the Twelve Steps of Alcoholics Anonymous, I wondered what the Catholic Church thought of them. Through my research, I learned of Father Ed Dowling, SJ, a Jesuit priest who had noticed similarities between St. Ignatius's Spiritual Exercises and the Twelve Steps. When Fr. Dowling met Bill Wilson, a cofounder of Alcoholics Anonymous (along with Dr. Bob Smith), the two of them became friends. Later, Bill called Fr. Dowling his spiritual advisor. Father Dowling was instrumental in the church's eventual acceptance of the Alcoholics Anonymous program.

I began to explore Ignatian spirituality and discovered it could help me go much deeper with my twelve-step program. It helped heal my vision of God. I began to understand why it had been hard for me to trust him with all that was happening. Through these approaches to prayer, my ability to trust God grew enough to hand over our situation to him—all of it. That is when things got better.

I have found that these two tools—the Twelve Steps and Ignatian spirituality—work hand in hand. Yet, I cannot believe how few people know about these wonderful gifts in our church's history.

———

Ultimately, my personal journey through the Twelve Steps and their connection to Ignatian spirituality led me to write this book. I want to establish right off the bat that I am not a psychologist, a psychiatrist, or an addictions counselor. I am not a theologian, a religious, or a philosopher. I am simply a Catholic mom who has walked through the trenches of addiction and is seeking to share her experience, her strength, and her hope with you. My twelve-step program teaches me that I cannot tell you how to fix your loved one. But it does encourage me to share my experience, knowing that God, through the Holy Spirit, will help you by giving you just the right nugget of truth you need when you need it.

There are some things I wish I'd known when I was the parent of a child in high school or middle school. But would I have been able to hear those things then? I believe that God, who gives us free will, opens our ears to hear him when, and only when, we are ready. So, if that is where you find yourself, please join me in this journey.

If you are the parent or grandparent of a teenager or soon-to-be teenager and are scared of what lies ahead, I want you to walk along beside me. Let me be your companion. I'll share with you the tools I have gathered along this path that have helped me to find peace. God will be with us, and he does not want us to be afraid.

If you are a son or daughter of an alcoholic, a brother or sister, an aunt or uncle, or a friend of someone whose disease has fractured relationships that you hold dear, know that it is never too late and that hope is always available.

If you are a teacher, mentor, or friend looking to be informed about this disease, join me as we bravely shine a light on it. We will meet some amazing people. I think you will be surprised at the gifts our church has to offer that can be useful as we face this age-old problem. My experience of the research has been like a great archeological dig. I have stumbled upon wonderful tools in our church's history. Through those searches, I've learned from priests and saints who have helped me find the serenity I need, no matter my situation.

My goal is to offer first aid. I want to give you a life vest that you can wear until you are brave enough to reach out to a twelve-step group, to your priest, or to a counselor on your own. I remember being so afraid of stepping into the recovery section of a bookstore that I would wait for the aisle to clear before selecting a book from its shelves. Then, I would tuck the book between two others before checking out at the register. If you are in that same place, I want to walk beside you through this book and remind you that you are not alone. There is hope.

Addiction is an isolating disease, and my twelve-step program says we are only as sick as our secrets. I think it's time we, as a church, had a discussion about the disease of addiction. Let's have a long conversation about it and ask honest questions. Let's take a fresh look at addiction, going beyond the dramatic headlines or scenes on television, and consider what we can learn from this disease and recovery that will help our families cope, grow, and heal.

STEP ONE

Powerless

We admitted that we were powerless—that our lives had become unmanageable.
—Step One of the Twelve Steps

He who goes about to reform the world must begin with himself, or he loses his labor.
—St. Ignatius of Loyola

When I walked into my first twelve-step meeting on a hot and muggy August day in 2010, I was scared and depressed. I wasn't there because I wanted to be. I was there because I had run out of options. As soon as I entered the room, I recognized a lady from church. I didn't know her personally, but she reached out a hand and asked, "Is this your first meeting?" When I told her that it was, she said, "I'm so glad you're here."

I lost count of the number of times that people said that phrase to me: "I'm so glad you're here." Though it sounded like a rote greeting you might get if a twelve-step meeting had a drive-through window, I learned that every person there had lived some version of my story. They knew what it took to arrive at and walk through that door.

I remembered the lady from church because her husband had passed out in the pew in front of us one Sunday, and several people, including my husband, had rushed to call an ambulance—only for the man to refuse to be checked once he came around. His wife had seemed odd to me that day. She was praying on the kneeler when he passed out. When she saw him, she eased back into the pew, put her arm around him, and whispered into his ear until he regained consciousness. After that, as though nothing had happened, she slipped back onto the kneeler and continued praying.

Who does that? I wondered. *Why isn't she doing something?* If it had been me, I would have gone into full panic mode. Yet she seemed calm. *She has to be nuts*, I thought.

I recalled that memory as I stood in the basement room of that little church on that first meeting day, still in disbelief that this was my life. I don't think she remembered me. And even if she did, it no longer mattered. I now had to face the truth.

Powerless

I guess things have to get really bad before many of us are willing to reach out for help. If you are holding this book in your hand, then you probably know something about the courage it took for me to overcome my shame and walk into that meeting. The shame associated with drugs and alcohol had taught me to keep my mouth shut for a long time. In fact, my shame was so pervasive that I hadn't allowed even the possibility that my son suffered from drug and alcohol addiction to enter my thoughts until there was no way to deny it any longer. Just three days earlier, I had put him into a rehabilitation center for the first time.

I arrived at that first meeting desperate, pleading with God to help me find a way to fix my son. I was lost and questioning everything I had ever believed to be true about myself. Our family was out of control. My son was in rehab, my two girls seemed shell-shocked, our business was struggling, and my husband and I were not getting along. What was God thinking, sending me this mixed-up little woman from church? I thought I needed a professional to help me figure things out. If I could just make it through that one-hour meeting, I would never darken that door again. I did not want to be a member of this club.

When the meeting started, the chairperson opened it with the Serenity Prayer:

> God, grant me the serenity to accept the things I cannot change,
> courage to change the things I can,
> and wisdom to know the difference.

I had heard that prayer before—maybe on a television show where the program had a scene that involved a twelve-step meeting. I'd dismissed it as irrelevant to my life. Now I listened to the words and realized it brought a little calm to my otherwise manic thoughts. Perhaps for the first time, I received a bit of direction. The little prayer awakened me to the notion that I didn't have to carry this burden alone. It helped me sort my problems into two categories: those I had control over and those I would hand over to God, thus cutting my problems in half.

Still, I felt twitchy. I was so uncomfortable. I wanted to leave. The group was small enough that we were able to sit around a table. I could not sneak out without being noticed. So, I stayed.

After the chairperson read the opening statement that explains how the meeting works, we went around the room and introduced ourselves by first name only. Anonymity is a big part of most twelve-step programs. It allows each person, and especially any newcomers, to feel safe enough to share, if that is what they want to do.

Then we read the Twelve Steps. Here again was something I'd heard about before but had never actually read. Each person around the table took a turn reading a step, and I was struck by how spiritual each one sounded. Step Three describes having "made a decision to turn our will and our lives over to the care of God, *as we understood*

Him." Step Eleven says that we "sought through prayer and meditation to improve our conscious contact with God *as we understood Him*, praying only for knowledge of His will for us and the power to carry that out."

I had no idea the Twelve Steps were so spiritual.

As I listened to each one, I realized my son needed what the Twelve Steps taught. Even though we'd always gone to church and my kids went to Catholic schools, I felt spirituality was a big part of what was missing in his life. This program might be okay after all.

It's been ten years since that first meeting, and I cannot remember the topic we covered that day. What I do remember is that the women around that table gently suggested it was *me* I needed to take care of, not my son. It was *I* who needed to use these twelve steps. They talked about how they "worked the steps" in their own lives. Again, that seemed strange. Wasn't my son the one with the problem? Everything seemed backward then. Yet the more they talked about taking care of themselves, the more I realized how appealing that sounded.

Like many moms, I considered the needs of my husband and kids first. Taking care of myself seemed selfish. I watched my mother care for others to the detriment of her own health. But wasn't that what I was supposed to do? These ladies asked me to look at the long-term cost of caring for others without caring for myself. They asked me to consider what I was modeling for my children about self-care. And somewhere deep inside, I knew this to be true. Their comments felt like permission.

In that one hour, I felt calm. Maybe I felt a bit of peace, too. Both of those feelings had been absent from my life for so long, I couldn't remember how much I needed them. I knew there was something of value for me there. I could not put my finger on it, but it was mysterious and wonderful. By the meeting's end, I knew I would go back. I needed more.

The Catholic Connection

Today I can tell you that the Twelve Steps of Alcoholics Anonymous have transformed my life. My son's addiction was the impetus for change in our family. We are better people because of the adjustments we've made working our twelve-step programs.

Even so, while I knew there was something special about the program in that first meeting, I wanted to be careful of how I approached things dealing with this disease. The stakes were very high. I eventually learned that for an addict or alcoholic, there are only three possible paths. As they say in the program, an addict can get sobered up, locked up, or covered up—in other words, he or she can choose recovery, go to jail or a mental institution, or die. Those are the only three options. I wanted to be sure I followed a true and safe path.

I went home and began to research the Alcoholics Anonymous (AA) program. I already shared in the introduction that I wanted to be sure AA didn't go against the teachings of the church. That's how I stumbled upon the name of Ed Dowling, SJ, the Jesuit priest who became friends with Bill Wilson, a cofounder of AA. Father Dowling noticed the similarities between the Twelve Steps and the *Spiritual Exercises of St. Ignatius of Loyola*. When Father Ed and his Jesuit brothers first read the book, *Alcoholics Anonymous*, sometimes referred to as the *Big Book* because the paper used in the first edition was so thick, they noticed that the Twelve Steps even appeared in the same order as Ignatius's Spiritual Exercises.

When Fr. Ed made his first trip to New York to meet Bill W., Bill thought the fellow who appeared at his door on that late winter night was another drunk. Then Bill noticed the Roman collar when Fr. Ed removed his coat. Father Ed introduced himself and began to talk with him about the chart he and his fellow Jesuit brothers had hung on a wall, comparing the Twelve Steps and the Spiritual Exercises. Bill W. later said, "In my abysmal ignorance, I actually inquired,

'Please tell me—who is this fellow Ignatius?'" Years later, Fr. Raymond Kennedy, SJ, secured Bill W. as a speaker at the National Clergy Conference on Alcoholism, and Bill included in his talk the following statement: "While of course the Twelve Steps of Alcoholics Anonymous contain nothing new, there seems no doubt that this singular and exact identification with Ignatian Exercises has done much to make the close and fruitful relation that we now enjoy with the Church."

St. Ignatius believed, just as Step One says, that change needs to begin with ourselves. As quoted above, St. Ignatius taught that "he who goes about to reform the world must begin with himself, or he loses his labor." For me, that sums up the entire twelve-step program. We change the world by changing ourselves first. That is the best place to start our journey.

Step One says, "We admitted that we were powerless—that our lives had become unmanageable."

What It Means to Be Powerless

Step One is comprised of two components. The first part says that we are powerless. For me to properly understand what that means, I need to know how the word *power* is defined. Merriam-Webster Dictionary defines *power* as "the ability to act or produce an effect" or "possession of control, authority or influence over others." If I am to admit that I have no power over my loved ones who suffer, then I acknowledge and accept that there is no action I can take upon them that will change the choices they make for themselves.

The second part of Step One is easy for most families to accept. It says that life has become "unmanageable." It is this portion of Step One that typically leads us to seek help. Our family tried everything to change our addicted loved one. Every single person became hyper-focused on his behavior. Still, the insanity continued. We were as sick and tired as he was of our situation.

The lady who met me at the door of that first meeting, whom I will call Annie, told me that the short version of Step One is "I can't." I love that version because it's simple. When I repeat it to myself, I don't overthink the point. *I can't.* To me, it means I can't change another person. I can't fix a situation. I can't make it all go away, no matter how hard I try. I simply cannot. I cannot play God. I can't keep trying to be God. The point of Step One is admitting the truth of this.

My first thought after reading Step One was, *No problem.* I knew my life was unmanageable. I knew I had no control over alcohol or the addict in my life. I felt sure I had Step One down already. But was it really that straightforward? I eventually came to realize that while I understood the *concept* of Step One, I had not yet learned how to live out the truth of it. I didn't realize how many hidden intentions lurked beneath the surface of my actions.

When I managed my adult son's affairs, was I doing it for his benefit or my own? When I called and checked on him several times a day, did he feel better, or was I doing it so that *I* felt better? Was he relieved when I heard his voice and learned he was okay, or did *I* need relief and my own nerves calmed? As I asked myself these questions, the answers were obvious. I started to see that many times my actions had ulterior motives.

As I began to think about the concept of powerlessness, I thought about those early scenes in Genesis 3. Just before Eve had tasted the fruit, Satan began to sow doubt into her mind when he offered that first lie in verse 5: "For God knows that when you eat of it your eyes will be opened, and you will be like God." Could it be that deep down, we all still buy into that idea?

For alcoholics, there is no power over alcohol. They can try to only drink beer, or only drink after 5:00 p.m. They will often set up arbitrary rules to try to help themselves control their drinking. Under their own willpower they will always fail because drinking, for the alcoholic, is a compulsion. And, a *compulsion* is defined by Oxford Languages as "the action or state of forcing or being forced to do something" or "an irresistible urge to behave in a certain way, especially against one's conscious wishes."

Father Fred Harkins, SJ, who wrote *Father Fred and the Twelve Steps: A Primer for Recovery*, describes the proper use of willpower in his taped talks that were later printed into book form: "I realized that I have to have will power. It says in the 'Big Book' that the place for the legitimate use of will power is the suggestions, the steps, the slogans, the suggestions we get from other members—especially from our sponsor. Will power will work there. But I came to learn that my will power against alcohol and other drugs is of no avail. It cannot do the job."

I began to see the paradox of this work. Just as the disease of addiction tells subtle lies to feed itself, lies that convince the addict he or she cannot live without the drink or drug, I have a disease that feeds itself too. My disease creeps in when I count bottles or pills. It's operating when I beg, argue, or try to reason with the addict in my life. If I hide keys or bottles or money, I'm catering to the disease by trying to manipulate the situation, inserting myself into it. My own disease tells me I have control. When I believe my disease, I am not owning my powerlessness. I am as sick as my loved one. I, too, have a disease that needs the help of the Twelve Steps.

When our opening reading says, "Our thinking becomes distorted by trying to force solutions, and we become irritable and unreasonable," it describes the typical family member who comes into the rooms (a phrase used to provide anonymity for twelve-step meetings) for the first time. To live in the truth of Step One, I needed to recognize that all those things I tried in order to control my son did not influence the outcome of my situation. In fact, they tended to get in the way of the work God was doing with my loved one. They also kept me busy focusing on everyone but myself. It was important for me to see and then accept that I was—and always will be—powerless over another person. Until I could accept that, I could not move forward.

Part of learning powerlessness is *un*learning our attempts to fix our loved ones or get them healed faster. The twelve-step program is very gentle towards us. Every person is allowed to understand the concept of each step in his or her own time. And just as God gives us free will, we must learn to respect that he has given our addicted loved ones free will as well. Who are we to interfere?

They say alcoholics and addicts often have to "hit bottom" before they are willing to get help. When you are at the bottom, with no place to go, that is when you are most likely to reach out for help. That is when a person recognizes and begins to accept his or her powerlessness. By the time I arrived at the meeting on that summer day, I felt I had hit my own bottom. I had tried many things to change my family's situation and nothing had worked. In fact, things had only gotten worse. My life had become unmanageable.

One day I stopped to purchase some gasoline. When I went inside to pay for it, I noticed the convenience store sold hookahs and bongs, which are used to smoke marijuana. I was furious. I decided to take pictures to send them to the local paper to announce to the world what was being sold there.

I look back and wonder why I did that. Why did I think that action was going to make a difference in my son's life? You see, it is legal for paraphernalia to be sold in convenience stores in my state, so long as a sign is posted near those items that states they are not to be used with illegal substances. It was not illegal for the store to sell those items, but it *was* illegal for me to take pictures of them without permission. And while all of that seems rather absurd, the main point is that my actions were going to do little to change my family's situation.

I snapped those pictures with the owner yelling at me, asking me what I was doing. When I headed back out to my car, he followed me, grabbed my arm, and tried to force me back into the store. I was scared by that point and decided I would not let him take me inside. Instead, I deleted the pictures, just as he told me to, so he would let go of me.

When I got into my car, my hands shook so hard that I had trouble driving. I realized that if I was willing to do something that crazy to avoid dealing with my problems, I needed help. It was as if I cried "Uncle!" at that moment.

In Step One, we must come to that place of surrender, just as our addicted loved ones do. And we must be given the space to do it in our own time.

This idea was understood early in the AA movement. Dr. William Duncan Silkworth, referred to as "the little doctor who loved drunks," is estimated to have treated over 40,000 alcoholics in his lifetime. He was a graduate of Princeton University and New York University's Bellevue Medical School. He theorized that problem drinkers would have to learn to accept that it was impossible for them to tolerate alcohol. He counseled Bill W. to stop preaching to drunks and to instead share that their situation was hopeless. He felt that only once they knew that they were powerless over alcohol would they then be open to a spiritual remedy.

Dr. Silkworth was not the only one who held this belief. The psychiatrist Carl Jung was among the first in his field to understand that alcoholism should be approached from a spiritual angle. In a 1961 letter to Bill W., Jung said, "Alcohol in Latin is 'spiritus.' You use the same word for the highest religious experience as well as for the most depraving poison. The helpful formula therefore is 'spiritus contra spiritum.'" This saying is often translated to mean that "high spirit counters low spirit." If a substance or drink is being used to make us feel better, then it is a poor substitute for a connection to the only One who can make us feel loved, which is an instant remedy to help us feel better.

Bill W. had learned this for himself, too. He had been hospitalized many times for his alcoholism. The last time he was hospitalized, the doctors told him he would probably not survive the next hospitalization. He later shared in an interview, "I was an agnostic, an atheist on top of it." As he lay in his hospital bed, aware of his limitations to heal on his own, he called out, "If there be a God, let him show himself." And that is when he felt God's presence and never doubted his existence again. It was also when his sobriety began.

St. Ignatius of Loyola had his own version of this experience. He was a soldier wounded in battle, but as his wounds began to heal, they weren't healing properly. His vanity led him to go back to his doctors and have them rebreak his leg so it could heal without blemish. He asked for books with great stories of knights in battle and romance to read during his convalescence, but the only books available told about Jesus and the lives of the saints.

Ignatius could not change his life by himself. He also could not continue on as he had before. As he read those spiritual books about Jesus and the saints, Ignatius began to pay attention to his feelings. He was surprised to find these stories captivating his attention, leaving him with feelings of joy. This was not so much a "rock bottom" moment as a time of realizing God was at work within him, leading him towards a new way of being, or proceeding, in his life. He only needed to accept the invitation.

The commonalities in all of these stories—including mine—are the moments of becoming aware of God and his work in our lives. In our poverty of power, we began to believe there might be a way other than our own. To me, this is what conversion looks like.

Furthermore, this source of love was able to show us a way out that we could not see on our own. The feeling is so large that it cannot be described with words. It can only be sensed in and through a life converted. Something changes. Hope is given. The yoke is lifted. Only God can do this.

Let me hasten to add that when I say I was changed forever, I don't mean I was cured. Like my addicted loved ones, I have only a daily reprieve. I must get up each day and remember again that "I can't." I must plug into the One who can.

Once I understood my true powerlessness and accepted it, I came to see the lady from church, Annie, in a new light. She knew the secret of which responsibilities belonged to her and which ones she would hand over to God. She did what she could do, and she hit the kneeler to ask for help with the things she couldn't.

Now I know who the mixed-up lady really was.

WORK THE STEP

Begin by finding a quiet, comfortable spot where you can acknowledge God's presence.

- Read and meditate on Psalm 8.
- Make a list of the ways you have tried to change another person or situation. List the outcomes of your efforts to "help" others.
- What do you think or fear would happen if you considered relinquishing your power to God and truly trusting him with your loved one?
- List the ways that your life has become unmanageable because of the addiction of a friend or family member.
- What are a few ways that you might reach out for help?
- Read John 16:32–33. Notice how Jesus reminds us that our peace is in him.

End this time of personal encounter with God by praying the prayer below or one of your own.

Heavenly Father, I come to you today with a scattered and anxious mind. I ask that you help me to become aware of my actions. Please help me to be present enough in my day to notice the motivations that lie beneath my actions. Help me to acknowledge that the only power I have is to offer my situation to you. Console my heart and guide my day. Amen.

STEP TWO

A Power Greater Than Ourselves

Came to believe that a Power greater than ourselves could restore us to sanity.

—Step Two of the Twelve Steps

Act as if everything depended on you; trust as if everything depended on God.

—St. Ignatius of Loyola

After my first meeting, even though the entire program felt odd to me, I continued to go back. The people there seemed to have their own secret language. No one offered any direct advice. When I would share, many of them would nod and smile and then offer an affirmation such as, "You're in the right place" or "Keep coming back."

They were an eclectic group of people. Some were older than I was, some were younger. One person had a mental or emotional disability. They represented a variety of occupations and socioeconomic levels. I didn't know their religion or political persuasions. As a rule, we tend to surround ourselves with individuals who are most like us—the people in this group weren't anything like me.

In the beginning, I was uncomfortable with the group. I didn't know how to be myself. I didn't know how to accept others as they were. But after a bit of time and the sharing of experiences, I saw how irrelevant those things were. I came to see their souls rather than the packages they were housed in.

As we took turns sharing in the group, I realized that I was learning a lot of important things from the woman with the disability. If I listened closely, I could receive a message from each person there that would relate to my situation. I watched the other women to see how they responded to what people shared. I was on the lookout for condescending glances or looks of shock. Instead, I found that they looked with love at each person who was willing to bare her heart to the group. They were able to see something I didn't yet know to recognize. I was so accustomed to being on guard against the ever-present judgment that comes with addiction that I did not trust enough to look below the surface.

Over time, I learned that we come to see people in the group as instruments of God. And as we progress, we begin to see through a lens of mercy instead of judgment. More importantly, if we pay close attention, we are able to find God seated around the table with us, many times in the person we might have considered the most unlikely or in the one who is suffering the most.

These women began to open my mind to a different idea of God.

Who Is the God of My Understanding?

Step Two is the one that most directly speaks of our connection with God. It says we "came to believe that a Power greater than ourselves could restore us to sanity." Let's talk first about the "Power greater than ourselves" language. What does that mean? For me, it means the Christian God. But for some people it can mean something else entirely.

Truthfully, I was at first offended by the phrase "a Power greater than ourselves." I felt they should just say "God" and be done with it. But that was a selfish and misguided thought. After all, twelve-step meetings are open to believers and nonbelievers alike, and a lot of hurt people come into the rooms of these meetings. They have often been scarred by people who were religious in word but not in deed. These rooms become places where hurt people can heal in their own time and in their own way.

I watched many times as someone new would come to a meeting and say, "I don't believe in God." An old-timer would usually say, "That's all right. I'm so glad you're here." Over time, I began to imagine that perhaps Jesus would do the same. Then the member would ask, "Do you believe that that chair can hold you up?" The newcomer, usually looking a little confused, would say *yes*. "Then let that be your higher power for today," the member would say. That suggestion for the newcomer to substitute the chair for a god they may or may not have believed in seemed so strange and even sacrilegious to me early on. I came to see that this program begins by helping people who are hurt learn to believe in something small. Later I would hear them say, "It doesn't matter who your higher power is, as long as it's not you."

That statement was eye-opening, for me. It made me realize that when I eased God out of a situation to do my own will, I was, in fact, trying to be the god of my understanding. And what does that say about my beliefs? One twelve-step friend says that when he begins to feel anxious, he has to look and see if he's misplaced his dependence. Putting our dependence on God is the real work of Step Two.

The program challenged me to open my mind beyond the ideas that I had grown up with. It seemed obvious that God was greater than I was. But did I *really* believe he was? This reminds me of how we see an airplane flying high overhead. It is but a small speck moving across the sky while in flight. Once it lands and rolls into the gate, we can see its true size and are astounded by how large it is. Are we close enough to God to understand his true power and size?

Father Ed Dowling once gave a talk at the 1955 St. Louis convention of Alcoholics Anonymous about our idea of God. He said that we need to move from an obscure and confused idea of God to a more distinct one. He also said that as humans, our thoughts of God will always be lacking. He compared our human understanding of God to the old German saying: "Very few of us know how much we have to know in order to know how little we know."

As I moved into Step Two, I began to think it might be good to release some of my old ways of thinking about God and open my mind to what I could learn from others. Because, as in my initial reading of Step One, I felt Step Two was behind me from the start—that it was already done. I believed in God and I always had. I could move on.

Except you can't move on. Not until you "come to believe," as the step says, which suggests it is a process. In fact, it is a process that ultimately gives us the ability to trust to the degree required of us in Step Three. And it never comes in an instant. It comes only through time spent with our Lord, or God "as we [understand] Him."

The new terminology about "the God of our understanding" made me question my understanding of God. What did that mean to me? Intellectually, I knew that God is love. That's what it says in the Scriptures. But did I truly believe that? I'd always been told I was made in God's image, but did I accept that as my birthright? Had I instead formed God into *my* image? I also thought about anthropomorphism—where we assign human emotions or characteristics to animals or inanimate objects. Because we are limited individuals, we don't have the vocabulary or insight needed to properly describe God. Unless you have spent time with God, how can you really know him or even be able to describe him?

I grew up in the Southern Baptist denomination and was taught that you invite Jesus into your heart to be your personal Lord and

Savior, and then the deal is done. You're destined to go to heaven once you die. But I never trusted that idea. It seemed too easy. I always had so much doubt. Perhaps that is why I eventually started searching.

Many years ago, I suggested to my husband that we attend the Rite of Christian Initiation as Adults (RCIA) in the Catholic Church. This class teaches people who are interested in the Catholic faith the beliefs of the Catholic Church and what they are based upon. When the class is finished, they decide whether or not they want to enter the church. When I first proposed this idea, I think he thought that I'd lost my mind. I asked him to attend one class and form his own opinion. One class turned into two, and before we knew it, Easter Sunday had come, and we had joined the universal church. I liked the Catholic Church for many reasons. One was how the church was connected to Jesus throughout its history in a way the Protestant church was not. I also loved how every event in our lives was celebrated around the Mass. That felt right to me.

All my life, I knew something greater than we could imagine had to have created this big, beautiful, mixed-up world we live in. But I had never come to know "my personal Lord and Savior" intimately. I knew I should have; I just didn't know how.

Truthfully, I think I was afraid of God. I felt unworthy. I had done a lot of things wrong in my life. I also was scared of what God's will might look like. I didn't have enough experience with the God of my understanding to know how trustworthy he was. More important, I had formed an idea in my mind of God as being "police-like" in nature. When an adult tells you, "God won't like it if you do that . . ." you start to shy away from the notion of God without knowing that, by believing what that adult told you, you've unconsciously created a false one, who acts as the disciplinarian.

I didn't know who my Creator really was or how to get to know him. And when you don't know someone very well, do you trust him?

When things got complicated, it became clear that I had a lot of work to do. My lack of trust in God especially showed itself when I faced my son's addiction. For the longest time, rather than facing the reality of the life-threatening disease gripping my son by turning to my loving, omnipotent, heavenly Father, I denied the existence of the problem. Then I took actions against a local convenience store that sold drug paraphernalia. It didn't make any sense. I was reacting to my situation but didn't know what to do. Slowly, I began to realize that my vision of God was distorted and that I had no idea who he really is.

Opening Up to a New Image of God

Two things eventually helped open my mind to a different image of God. The first was a book a friend gave me, written by Greg Boyle, SJ, called *Tattoos on the Heart*. Father Greg is a Jesuit priest who established the largest gang rehabilitation center in the world. The organization he runs, Homeboy Industries, helps rehabilitate gang members by offering drug and alcohol programs, classes related to the GED and on anger management, and tattoo removal, among other things. They also give jobs that have former gang members working side by side with former members of rival gangs. Father Greg discovered that once these former gang members saw the humanity of another person, there was no way they could continue to see each other as enemies.

In the first chapter of *Tattoos on the Heart*, Father Greg tells the story of a father and son he knew. The son was taking care of his father, who was now advanced in years. Each night the son read to his father in an effort to help him drift off to sleep. But the father would not close his eyes. He could not take his eyes off the son he loved so much. Father Greg likened this father's devotion to his son to God's love for us. This theme of God loving us more than we can imagine is a common thread that runs throughout the book. As I set out to work Step Two and read this account, it occurred to me that I had never thought of God in that light. I'd read the Scriptures about God's love for us, but because I'd always been told what God would and would not like, I had primarily fashioned him into some sort of enforcer.

The second thing that happened to change my image of God took a while for me to fully see. I was asked to help another twelve-step member take a meeting into the county jail for a semester of classes. I had never been inside a jail, but it sounded intriguing. I decided to give it a try and really enjoyed our meetings there. It helped keep my focus off of my addicted loved ones, and I decided to continue volunteering.

The next semester the jail chaplain asked me to teach another class, entitled "Moral Reconation Therapy," a form of cognitive behavioral therapy. I didn't have a clue what that was, but the chaplain assured me I was capable enough to figure it out. It was required for some of the inmates so they could regain their driver's licenses once their sentence was over. I was given a copy of the course book and got busy trying to understand it. The course offered seventeen steps that each inmate needed to take to "escape their own prison." I was cautioned that until the first of the seventeen steps was completed, they should not move on. The first step was being truthful.

Eleven women were enrolled in the class, and on the first day I asked, "How many of you have a problem with drugs and alcohol?" I knew that each of their charges was connected to drugs and alcohol, but only three hands went up in the air.

I was dumbfounded: "Really?" They began to give me a lot of legalistic responses.

I continued, "All eleven of you find yourselves in this county jail. Alcohol and drugs happen to be the ticket that got you into this place. And only three of you have a problem?"

It astounded me that they could not see that they had a problem. But then that little book began to educate me as much as it did them. In fact, the lesson contained in that book changed my life, and I hope theirs, too. The lesson was this: *Our beliefs inform our attitudes, and our attitudes influence our behavior.*

Let me illustrate this for you. Let's say that when I was a child, my brother told me I was ugly. And since children often taunt their siblings, let's say he told me this many times. After a while, I would begin to believe him. This would make me lose my self-esteem. I might feel less secure about the person I was. And since I felt bad about the way I looked, I might start to dress in a dowdy manner so I wouldn't call attention to my appearance. I might walk with poor posture and keep my head down. I would believe I was ugly. That belief would inform my attitude towards myself, and that attitude would influence my behavior.

But was that original belief true? The whole thing was based on misinformation.

In the same way, the women in my class thought they didn't have a drug problem because they misunderstood what a drug problem was. In the past, they had been able to stop using. This made them think they had power over the drug or drink. But the use of drugs and alcohol had created problems in their lives—maybe caused them to have an automobile accident that landed them in jail, separated them from their children, and loaded them up with expensive legal and automobile repair bills.

Why couldn't they see it as a drug or alcohol problem? Perhaps because their perception of the truth had been formed as a way to protect themselves.

In the same way, we need to consider our beliefs about God when we come to Step Two. What do we truly believe about God? What is the basis for those beliefs? Where did those beliefs come from in our life? And are they based on the truth?

The idea that God wanted to scold me for my transgressions kept me from turning to him in my time of need. How could I ask for help if I believed he would be too disappointed in me to hear my prayers? I believed God was most concerned with the ways I'd fallen short. I didn't believe God loved me so much that he couldn't take his eyes off of me, so I kept my distance. I didn't think I had any other option. This led me to try to handle the situation myself.

Even in AA's formation, there was some question about the language used in describing this power greater than ourselves. In Ernst Kurtz's *Not-God: A History of Alcoholics Anonymous*, a conversation is related between Bill W. and Fr. Ed Dowling, SJ, regarding some phrasing in Step Twelve that left the idea of God unclear. "There was a move afoot within the fellowship just then, he told Dowling, to change the phrase in the Twelfth Step to 'spiritual awakening'—it seemed to Bill an attempt to mask rather than clarify the role of the divine in the alcoholic's salvation. Tartly, Father Ed offered a succinct response: 'If you can name it, it's not God.'"

It's not easy to put words to this power that is greater than myself. I was beginning to look beneath the words that I had commonly used in trying to understand God. When we had taken my son to a twelve-step immersion program, the counselor met with us to report on his progress.

"How is he doing?" we asked.

"Well, he's being honest but not very truthful," the counselor said.

"What's the difference?" I asked.

"The truth is what is real. Honesty is our *perception* of the truth."

I came to realize that my vision of God had been marred. That misunderstanding had created the distance in my relationship with him. I would say I believed in God and he was all powerful, and I was being honest when I said those things. But the *truth* was that I didn't really believe. If I truly believed God was a power greater than myself, I wouldn't have tried to handle things alone. In my experience, this step requires the slow work of spending time alone with God, getting to know him.

Step Two says, "Came to believe that a Power greater than ourselves could restore us to sanity."

Building Trust

Eventually I came to see that Step Two was all about hope. Once I realized I was powerless in Step One, then I was given hope in Step Two. This is where a real relationship with God can begin.

My twelve-step friend Annie says the short version of Step Two is "God can." When I realize my powerlessness and remind myself that "I can't," then I am immediately offered the hope that "God can." And what can God do? He can restore me to sanity.

Like the women in the county jail, my thoughts, attitudes, and actions in the face of my son's addiction were not rational. I was unable to fight this battle on my own, even though I kept trying to do so. I was the picture of insanity. I needed time, prayer, and meditation as well as some blind faith in order to take a chance on God as I now understood him.

It reminds me of a story of a young horse on our farm. My husband, Matt, went out for a ride on our new and inexperienced horse we had named Bo. We bought him at an auction. He was gorgeous. But, like me, he was afraid of his shadow—and a big horse that is fearful can be dangerous. You need to build a relationship with that kind of horse so he trusts you enough to confront his fears.

That day a farmer had cut and baled hay into large, round rolls on the property adjacent to ours. When Matt took Bo out to the field, Bo startled and began snorting as soon as the first bale of hay came into view. If that thing could be run off, he was just the horse to do it. His ears twitched back and forth as he waited to hear if that thing would challenge him. Unsure, he backed away. For a little while, Matt let him retreat, and then he made a wide circle back around so Bo could see the bale again. But still, Bo wasn't budging. No matter how many circles Matt made, Bo refused to go near that bale of hay.

Finally, Matt got off Bo's back and walked in front of him, over to the bale of hay. He pulled a handful out of the center and offered it to him. Pleasantly surprised, Bo munched on the hay and then inched his way closer, sniffing and touching the hay for himself. Then Matt got on Bo's back and rode him away. Soon, they passed another bale. Again, Bo jumped, feet splayed in a position ready to take flight. Once again, Matt approached and then retreated in an effort to gain Bo's trust. Each time, it was a lesson for Bo that his rider would not take him into an unsafe situation.

Matt came home tickled by the day's lesson. He reported that Bo had to eat from eight bales of hay before he trusted that they weren't there to eat him. Finally, he could walk up to the hay without fear. We laughed at how silly this big fella was. Of course, our human understanding gave us more information than he was able to see or discern. He just needed to learn to trust that we would do what was best for him.

But I knew the same thing could be said for me. I needed to get to know my Creator better. I needed to see that he wouldn't lead me astray and leave me alone. I needed to experience that his will was always best for me. Being restored to sanity meant being brought into a trusting relationship with God.

Finding God in All Things

Saint Ignatius's conversion started out in a similar place. He needed to examine his ideas about God when his life changed too. Early on, he decided to sell his clothes, beg for food, and care for the sick and poor in an attempt to outdo the saints he'd read about. With prayer and meditation, he would come to see that those actions were not actually for God but for his own vanity.

Over time, he continued to pay attention. He started noticing the everyday miracles bestowed upon each of us. Ignatius came to believe God is active in our world. He started instructing the early Jesuits to go out and find God in all things. This became the signature spirituality of the Jesuits: *finding God in all things*.

This call to pay attention is something that helped me do the work of Step Two. As I began to pay attention, I began to see everyday gifts in a way I hadn't noticed before. I started keeping a list of the things I was grateful for, and I noticed many gifts. This new awareness helped paint a picture of a loving God. As I continued this practice, I realized that the good always outweighed the bad. Little by little, as I was able to read from the Scriptures about God's love for me and to accept it as true, I started to see the love and mercy of God more than the shame I had felt.

Saint Ignatius reminds us that if we look for God in all things, we can begin to recognize him for who he really is. That is just the thing I began to do in my effort to have a better understanding of him.

At twelve-step meetings friends would remind me, "God loves your son more than you ever could." The reality of my situation was that I didn't know God well enough to trust him with my son, at least not at the beginning. It was difficult to say that truth out loud, but now I know it was true.

Looking for God in all things, in the way St. Ignatius describes, became a powerful new tool. Just imagine the lessons we miss through our faulty perceptions of God or by being too busy to find God in all the everyday details of our lives! When we gain the awareness that "God can," there is relief in knowing we no longer have to try to deal with our situation on our own with our limited human means. Knowing that there is One who can deal with it gives us hope. And hope is a key ingredient in restoring our sanity.

WORK THE STEP

Begin by finding a quiet, comfortable spot where you can acknowledge God's presence.

- Read and meditate on Psalm 23.
- You may have read this psalm before. As you open your mind to a new idea of God, read it again. What did you notice this time?
- Create a list of ways you have seen and/or found God today.
- What things are you grateful for that you know are gifts from God today?
- Read Mark 8:27–29. In light of these verses, think how other people—your relatives and friends—might have conveyed their idea of God to you.
- How does your personal experience with God differ from those ideas? How is it the same?

End this time of personal encounter with God by praying the prayer below or one of your own.

Heavenly Father, I come to you today with an open space in my heart reserved just for you. Help me to release my old ideas of you that are inaccurate and to see you for who you really are. Help me to slow down and take notice of your fingerprints in the world. Give me what I need to navigate this day under your great care. Amen.

STEP THREE

Surrender

Made a decision to turn our will and our lives over to the care of
God as we understood Him.
—Step Three of the Twelve Steps

Take, Lord, and receive all my liberty,
my memory, my understanding,
and my entire will,
All I have and call my own.

You have given all to me.
To you, Lord, I return it.

Everything is yours; do with it what you will.
Give me only your love and your grace,
that is enough for me.
—Suscipe, St. Ignatius of Loyola

Even though I had attended meetings for several weeks, few people outside of our household knew our family secret. I did not want to cause any harm to our son. I understood the stigma that addiction carries.

One night, I decided to go to Mass at our church. Our parish was hosting a priest from the Fathers of Mercy congregation located in Auburn, Kentucky, not too far from the state line of Tennessee, my home state. I don't remember what the homily was about, and I didn't go to Mass with any agenda in mind. But afterwards, I held back from the crowd and waited for the priest. When I felt that there was a window of privacy, I walked up to him, shook his hand, and said, "Father, my son has a problem with drugs and alcohol. I don't know what to do."

He held onto my hand and said, "Wait just a minute, and we will have a talk." He continued speaking to the other parishioners until the last one left. Then he asked me to follow him into the confessional, where we could have some privacy.

"Let me share a story with you," he said as we sat down. "When I was young, but still living at home, I was a real troublemaker. I loved to pick fights. And I loved to drink. When I went out to drink, fighting always followed. My older brother was sick of me and the trouble that I was causing the family.

"One night, he knew that I had gone out to a bar, and because I had been arguing with another fellow, he knew that I was just itching for a fight. He went to our mother and said, 'Mom, I know which bar he went to. Why don't you go and drag him out of there? He will listen to you.'

"My mom looked at my brother and said, 'Son, I have a far better chance of fighting for your brother on my knees than I ever will by stepping one foot into that bar.'"

The father looked at me and smiled, spreading his arms wide open. "Look at me now. I am a priest of God."

There it was: crisp, clear instructions—laced with hope.

It wasn't that I hadn't been praying all along. Yet, when I looked closely at my intentions, I realized that my prayers were insurance—a back-up plan. In all honesty, what I really wanted was to be told what to do to fix the situation myself.

That night I realized that I was exhausted. I was tired of going it alone. His story helped me to become aware of my utter powerlessness over my family's situation. If I couldn't fix things, then maybe God actually could. This priest's mother had enough faith to place her son into the care of God. If I could find the courage, maybe I could too.

I left the confessional and found a quiet spot at the back of the church. Down on my knees, I uttered a simple prayer. I chose my words carefully. It was the beginning of my efforts to let go of my own will.

"Help him. Help me. Show me the way."

Step Three says, "Made a decision to turn our will and our lives over to the care of God."

The Three A's

Step Three is exactly what the priest's mother did—handed the problem of her son's behavior over to the care of God. She had the *awareness* necessary to comprehend that the problem was more than she or any human could handle and that God was the only answer. Her understanding of these facts came as the result of her *acceptance* of the current situation. Accepting our life, just as it is, means we consent to receive what is true and real. In other words, if I do not accept my situation as it is, I am living in a fantasy.

One of my husband's program mentors, Joe, had a platform of sorts, which became important to his sobriety. At the time when Joe found sobriety, AA's *Big Book* section titled "Acceptance Was the Answer," written by a physician, could be found on page 449 (third edition). He quoted this section so often that it earned him the name "449 Joe." (In the new fourth edition, it is found on page 417.) I love this statement because it illustrates the important role that acceptance plays in recovery for both the alcoholic and his or her family.

> Acceptance is the answer to *all* my problems today. When I am disturbed, it is because I find some person, place, thing, or situation—some fact of my life—unacceptable to me, and I can find

no serenity until I accept that person, place, thing, or situation as being exactly the way it is supposed to be at this moment. Nothing, absolutely nothing, happens in God's world by mistake. Until I could accept my alcoholism, I could not stay sober; unless I accept life completely on life's terms, I cannot be happy. I need to concentrate not so much on what needs to be changed in the world as what needs to be changed in me and in my attitudes.

I realized that I had to accept my powerlessness with action. If I was truly powerless and God was all powerful, then I would need to let go of any of my own efforts to change my son's situation. The *action* that was necessary for me to take was "letting go." That is the meat of Step Three. Specifically, it is what is meant by the phrase "Let go and let God." The priest's mom knew that she didn't have the power to help her son stop drinking. It was her *faith in action* that helped illustrate for me what it means to let go. She didn't hesitate.

In my twelve-step program, it is understood that the first three steps can be accomplished by utilizing these three A's: awareness, acceptance, and action. They are the guides that helped me to do the work of these three steps.

Once I am at the place of action, I go to our Lord in prayer and ask him to take my loved ones from my efforts. Then I leave the results to him. Twelve-steppers call that handing over *detachment*. Ignatius calls it *holy indifference*. If I hold on to outcomes, then any peace that I may have had from turning care over to God will be gone. My fellow twelve-steppers remind me, "Expectations are just premeditated resentments."

I've often heard people say, "Well, all we can do now is pray." They mean we have done all that we can do, and prayer is all that we have left. The problem with making that statement is that it seems to relegate prayer to the end of our options. It treats prayer as a last resort. With time and experience, I now realize the need for prayer comes first.

The short versions of Step One, "I can't," and Step Two, "God can," brings us to the surrender of Step Three: "I'll let him." According to Fred Harkins, SJ, the author of the book *Father Fred and the Twelve Steps: A Primer for Recovery*, the first three steps are the spiritual foundation that is made up of our own attitudes, thoughts, and decisions. He counsels others that a daily renewal of these ideas is required.

Every day, I need to remind myself of these three steps. They begin the process of restoring order by reconnecting my bond of dependence on God. In practical terms, they ask me to look outside of myself for help.

God's Assurance

If I had the power to fix my loved one, I probably would have already done it. Accepting that God is the only one who can help us out of our situation is the beginning. Each time that I take a step forward in blind faith, it allows my trust to grow. I have seen the fruits of trusting God. It is what is promised to us in Philippians 4:6–7: "Do not worry about anything, but in everything by prayer and supplication with thanksgiving let your requests be made known to God. And the peace of God, which surpasses all understanding, will guard your hearts and your minds in Christ Jesus."

I have been gifted with this peace a few times. One incident was so profound that I will always remember it as one of my closest encounters with God.

It was a time when we were trying to work out our boundaries with our son. We wanted to stop contributing to his disease, and we wanted to reserve our resources to help him if he ever chose to seek recovery. We took all financial means of help away, except paying his phone bill. We thought that we needed to keep that connection available to him, though a counselor reminded us that he could also use that connection to stay in contact with his source of drugs and alcohol. With that perception in mind, we decided that we would shut off his phone. It was one of the most difficult things that I'd ever done. I was basically cutting off my last bit of communication with my son. I would now be completely in the dark.

In making this decision, I had to acknowledge that paying for his phone was an action that I was taking for myself. If I was brutally honest, I did it so that I could call him and check on him whenever I wanted. In no way did this do anything to help him find recovery.

While I felt like I should cut this last tie, there was another voice whispering in my ear—*What if you are wrong?* Nevertheless, I went into my husband's office, pulled the file with the contact information for the phone company, and made the call. When I got the sales rep on the phone, she tried to discourage me from cancelling my contract early, telling me that there would be an early termination fee. I accepted responsibility for the fee, and the phone was turned off.

The thing that I dreaded most was a call from my son. I knew that he would call. He would find a way, and it wouldn't be pretty. You see, the disease of addiction will fight to stay alive. It will use any means it can to survive. I was very nervous in anticipation of that call.

My anxiety grew to the point that I had to leave the office and go home. As I made my way home, I could hardly believe what I had just done. What if it was the wrong thing to do? Our office was exactly seven miles from our home. I was lost in thought the entire drive. I switched between panicky thoughts and prayer, asking that God would help me do the right thing. I did not know what that right thing was.

Just when I was about to turn onto our road, something happened. It was as if something blinked in me. In that instant, a vision popped into my head. It was like a deposit was made into my bank of understanding. I was given the gift of knowing that I'd made the right choice.

In that same second, I had a deep understanding of our situation. I knew that what I did was an act of following God's will. My mind was directed to the story about King Solomon in 1 Kings 3:16–28, a Scripture passage that I didn't know well. But I knew that our situation had a profound connection to that story.

There were two women who lived in the same house, each of whom had an infant. One child died, and the women fought over the surviving child. They took their situation to King Solomon to make a judgment. In his wisdom, he flushed out the truth by offering to split the baby with his sword, giving each woman half. He knew that the real mother would love her child enough to give him up to save his life.

Cutting off communication with my son was an act of giving him up in the hope that he could survive his disease. I was taking my loved one and placing him fully into God's care. I knew that this was our only hope. I was certain. In that quiet moment on my drive home, I was given peace that surpassed all understanding. God had been there . . . if only for a second. It was enough.

I didn't worry for months. I didn't know where he was or what he was doing. I did know that he was right where he was supposed to be. It was a gift from God—one that I will never forget.

The Principle and Foundation

The spiritual foundation we build upon in the first three steps is essential. It seeks to repair the state of disorder that we find in our lives when we are facing an addiction or have a family member who is. Saint Ignatius's Spiritual Exercises begin with the First Principle and Foundation. Much like the first steps of AA, this stage seeks to move

God back into the center of our lives. It tells us that we are created for God, not the other way around. Because we are created for him, our lives should be a living testament to his will for us. When we lose our place, we become off-balance. This reorientation restores order that is needed to live our lives in harmony with God.

The First Principle and Foundation, as translated by Louis J. Puhl, SJ, states:

> Man is created to praise, reverence, and serve God our Lord, and by this means to save his soul.
>
> The other things on the face of the earth are created for man to help him in attaining the end for which he is created.
>
> Hence, man is to make use of them in as far as they help him in the attainment of his end, and he must rid himself of them in as far as they prove a hindrance to him.
>
> Therefore, we must make ourselves indifferent to all created things, as far as we are allowed free choice and are not under any prohibition. Consequently, as far as we are concerned, we should not prefer health to sickness, riches to poverty, honor to dishonor, a long life to a short life. The same holds for all other things.
>
> Our one desire and choice should be what is more conducive to the end for which we are created.

For me, the First Principle and Foundation is what the first three steps of AA hope to accomplish. Each of these tools is a reminder to us that God is our creator. He loves us more than we as humans can understand. The tall order of the First Principle and Foundation is intended to help us keep our eye on the prize. If we let God be in charge, our lives will be fruitful and our souls will be saved.

The writer Ernest Kurtz wrote his entire doctoral dissertation, which was later published as a book, on that same idea. He felt that the Twelve Steps of AA can be distilled down to one idea: the fact that we are not God. If I keep this idea, that I am not God, at the forefront of my mind, my spiritual foundation holds a little stronger.

The AA slogan "First Things First" helped me to be mindful of my place in the world. If we become attached or addicted to anything that gets in the way of God's plan for us or that is not useful to God's plan for us, we have become disordered, and chaos ensues.

Learning to Discern God's Will

Since we have made a decision to turn our lives and our will over to the care of God as we understand him, how can we be sure that what we are doing is in fact God's will? And can we be sure that what we have chosen is the best possible choice?

For me, these are the areas in which Ignatian Spirituality helps us the most. Ignatius has a lot to teach us about the process of discernment. He does this by teaching us to recognize the characteristics of the Spirit of God and those of the enemy and then to look at our intentions. He encourages us to consider our own motivations.

I relied on the book *God's Voice Within* by Mark Thibodeaux, SJ, to teach me these important principles. Discerning God's will and having the ability to make sound decisions carry a lot of weight when your loved one is wrestling with a life-threatening disease. Learning to recognize God's will is yet another avenue by which I get to know God. As I do this, I see just how much he loves and cares for me. Trust begins to grow. It is that trust that is necessary to make the decisions needed for healing.

During this time of turmoil as I was working on Step Three, I had been going to catechetical training classes to prepare myself to bring the twelve-step program to the county jail, which I mentioned earlier. While I wasn't teaching a catechism class, I wanted to be prepared in case anyone had questions about the faith. But I had to miss one class because we were taking my son to a twelve-step immersion program.

I decided to e-mail Sister Mary Michael, OP, who led the class, about why I had missed the session. I had decided that of all the people that I could let my guard down with, it was safe to do it with a sister. She responded to my e-mail by telling me that they would pray for my son and our family and that I could make up the session at another time. When I attended that makeup session, I remembered what I had emailed to sister—that I told her about our family situation.

Why did I do that? I wondered. I looked up, and it appeared as if Sister was looking my way. So, I did what any rational adult would do: I picked up a book and pretended to read.

I sat there for a minute, and then I glanced over my book to see if Sister was gone. I breathed a sigh of relief and then heard a quiet voice from behind me say, "Jean, how are you? And how is your son?" Sister's stealthy movement surprised me.

I had no time to think. So, this is what came out: "Sister, this has been the worst experience of my life. And yet, it has also been one of the best things to happen to our family. I can't explain it and don't understand it."

Sister's smile communicated that she understood what I was saying, even if I didn't. She patted my shoulder and said, "You must have asked to be so close to our Lord." Then she walked away just as quickly and quietly as she had arrived.

I must have asked to be so close to our Lord? What in the world was she talking about? I left dumbfounded and confused. That was nothing new.

It took me almost two years and a lot of twelve-step work to understand what she was saying. Now I see that when I pay attention, I keep God at the center. If I rely on him first and turn my will and my life over to him, God is *always there*. He is a constant presence in my days.

Most days before I even get up, I say, "What do I need to do today, Lord?" I lie there awhile in the quiet of my room and enjoy the peace that accompanies the sun's rising. If I remember to start there each day—putting God at the forefront of all I do—then order is restored. I am living out the First Principle and Foundation and doing the work of Step Three.

WORK THE STEP

Begin by finding a quiet, comfortable spot where you can acknowledge God's presence.

- Read and meditate on Psalm 40.
- Why do you think God gives us free will?
- What holds you back from giving up your will? List the reasons.
- Can you think of a time when you trusted God with a situation? What was the outcome? How did you feel "letting go"?
- Read Ephesians 6:5–8. Notice the gift of following God's will.

End this time of personal encounter with God by praying the prayer below or one of your own.

Heavenly Father, I am afraid to trust. Help me confront my fears. Help me let go of my loved ones and see and feel your love. Show me the path to healing for me and my family. Thank you for loving me enough to give me a choice. Amen.

STEP FOUR

Taking Stock

Made a searching and fearless moral inventory of ourselves.
—Step Four of the Twelve Steps

If we take an honest look at the mistakes we've made, we'll see that
many of them were a reaction to an unnamed fear within us.
—Mark Thibodeaux, SJ, *God's Voice Within*

Family night at our son's rehabilitation center demonstrated for us just how dysfunctional we had become. My husband was angry that I wasn't helping *him* deal with our situation. Our girls were upset that *they* had to go and witness their parents air our family's dirty laundry. And *I* was a weeping mess. You see, before our secret came out, I would have spent my time making my husband feel better. And, I would have kept quiet about the problems at home.

There was only one thing that I was sure of: I could no longer be the person I had been up to that point in our family arrangement. I didn't yet know who I was or how to live a healthy life. I had been in denial for a long time. Now that we had acknowledged the problem, I felt responsible for everything.

The counselor reminded me that I have three children and only one of them suffered from the disease of addiction. Still, I knew that I owned a part of our problem. I'd focused on a lot of exterior things—things the world considers important. Instead, I should have loved my son in a way that let him know it. I had contributed to his problem.

In the early days of attending my twelve-step program, my fellows in recovery tried to sell me on the idea of taking care of myself. While I did not know how to go about accomplishing that task, they continued to offer suggestions:

"Try to slow things down," one friend said.

"If you feel out of sorts, remember to 'H.A.L.T.' and ask yourself: 'Am I hungry, angry, lonely, or tired?'" another suggested. "Begin there with the basics."

Their words felt like permission to take care of myself. Even so, I wondered if they really knew what they were talking about. Wasn't that a selfish thing for a parent to do? As a wife and mother, my full-time job for the past twenty-three years had been making sure that the needs of four other people were always tended to. Since they were babies, my kids had come first. I had forgotten to stop at some point, look up, and see that they were all either grown or nearing adulthood. Even though they were progressing through different ages and stages, my response to that progression was either behind the curve or stagnated in a previous stage.

The social worker who led the family-night session suggested to me that I didn't cause my son's problem. She repeated the three C's of addiction: you didn't *cause* it, you can't *cure* it, and you can't *control* it.

"Maybe that is true," I said. But in my heart, I knew that my contribution was a factor. I needed to take ownership of our problems because I felt like I had a role in them.

"It reminds me of bacteria," I said. "If a wound isn't kept clean, then the conditions are ripe for the bacteria to thrive. If I do nothing to treat the wound, I've allowed them to fester and grow. Because I was too afraid to confront the problem in our home, the conditions were ripe for addiction to thrive and progress," I countered.

The counselor told me that I was being too hard on myself. I didn't believe her. I needed the truth. I needed it like I needed air to breathe. Finding the truth felt like I was taking action. I was taking a culture from our wound and learning what I should do next. I needed to know who or what was the source of our problems. I could not fight an unknown enemy.

Step Four says, "Made a searching and fearless moral inventory of ourselves."

Keep the Focus on Yourself

The first three steps help restore order between me and God. The next four steps are actions designed to restore order within me. Step Four asks me to simply take stock of my life. If I can remember to be objective and keep the focus on myself, I will be able to acknowledge that my actions are my own actions. I own them. Regardless of what another person has or has not done, I am still responsible for my response.

My sponsor once challenged me to speak about my problems using only the pronouns *I*, *me*, or *myself*. It was more difficult than I imagined. That exercise illuminated the fact that I knew more about the lives of family members than about my own.

I was really good at minding the business of others and doing it under the guise of "helping them out." In the case of my addicted loved ones, I fixed things that they should have fixed and paid bills that they should have paid themselves. I reminded them to get up and go to work. I made their responsibilities mine. Because I was taking care of their basic needs, they were able to continue their habit.

This kind of "help" evolves into behavior that is called *enabling*. This progressive focus on others eventually caused me to lose touch with myself. When my serenity depends upon the action of another person, I am what is referred to as *codependent*.

Addiction is a family disease. It touches every member of the family, because in family systems there is an unspoken code. We have rules and norms that we follow. When one member of the family steps outside of those parameters, other members jump in to ensure that the family system continues. Siblings of the addicted person end up holding more than their fair share of the responsibilities. They may feel that they need to protect their sibling and hide what he or she is doing. They can feel guilty or even resentful. Everyone in the family begins to assume more of his or her loved one's responsibilities.

As the family's focus shifts and boundaries blur, each member begins to lose his or her individual identity. The entire family works towards the mission of managing the life of the one who is suffering from an addiction. This is what psychologists refer to as *enmeshment*.

I was unable to look within until I separated myself from the system that evolved as a means of survival in our difficult situation. It was hard to believe that we didn't see what we were doing. Our counselor told us that enmeshment and enabling in these situations is a common occurrence.

"Let me tell you about the boiled frog," she said. "If you drop a frog in a pot of boiling water, he will jump out. But if you put a frog in cool water in a pot on the stove and gradually increase the temperature, he will boil alive and not realize what is happening until it is too late."

She helped us see that this is a progressive disease. Just as the problem with drugs and alcohol moves from use to abuse and from dependence to addiction, the family's role in the problem also gradually escalates. We become enslaved to maintaining and then fixing our loved ones.

Until we do the work of Step Four, we will be unable to form true partnerships with our families and others. Instead, we will either dominate them or depend on them too much. We will manipulate them and be self-centered. In this state, there is no sense of balance left in the family system. The work of Step Four is a practice that leads to self-discovery. It teaches me to keep the focus on myself and my actions. It is a reminder that I can only control myself. And to control myself, I must know myself.

There is a famous quote from the Chinese general Sun Tzu's book, *The Art of War*: "If you know the enemy and know yourself, you need not fear the result of a hundred battles. If you know yourself but not the enemy, for every victory gained you will also suffer a defeat. If you know neither the enemy nor yourself, you will succumb in every battle." In my battle for healthy relationships, it seemed odd that I would need to get to know who I was, until I realized how little I knew about myself.

One day after getting out of the shower, I felt something sore under my breast. It was just out of my line of vision, so I got out a compact mirror and saw a dark raised spot. *It must be another mole or skin tag*, I thought. I'd had a few of those and the dermatologist was never concerned about them. This spot was a little painful and my bra was rubbing against it, so I decided to cover it with a bandage until the soreness went away. For five or six days I dutifully covered and protected this spot. It didn't seem to get any better. In fact, it was getting more painful than before. Again, I got out my mirror and took a good look at the spot. I was stunned to see that it wasn't a skin tag at all; it was a tick.

Similarly, how easy it had been to dismiss things in my family that I'd considered small or insignificant, only to realize that they weren't small at all. Step Four helped me lay it all out so I could get an accurate picture of the good and the bad. I learned at a Jesuit retreat that St. Ignatius asks retreatants to look back in order to "draw profit." I loved that statement and wrote it down. His idea shifted my perspective of the work of Step Four from a negative to a positive one.

Before this shift, the work of Step Four felt punitive. As I began to heal the image that I held of God, I found compassion for myself and others. *Maybe this will move me closer to the "image" that I was created to be*, I thought.

With this new perspective, I was beginning to understand that God wasn't mad at me for falling short. He was sad that my sin was hurting me. My thoughts about this work began to align with the new understanding I had of God as a loving God.

I came to see the importance of examining myself. My new way of perceiving began to help me uncover the various ways that I had contributed to my son's disease. If I could learn what those actions were and replace them with something healing instead, then I was willing. And maybe this process would also help me discover who I really am.

There are two very important things to consider before you begin a Step Four inventory. The first is that in order for this step to be fruitful, you need to be completely truthful with yourself. The *Big Book* of Alcoholics Anonymous begins chapter 5, "How It Works," with this statement: "Rarely have we seen a person fail who has thoroughly followed our path. Those who do not recover are people who cannot or will not completely give themselves to this simple program, usually men and women who are constitutionally incapable of being honest with themselves."

The heart of twelve-step programs rests on the truth and our ability to see it for what it is. These programs were teaching a practical process that led me towards understanding a few basic ideas that I had never slowed down to consider before.

How often have our old beliefs and attitudes skewed our idea of truth? How many times did my ideas about what my adult son should or should not do get in our way? And are we qualified to offer judgment? I was challenged to see how limited our judgment can be when, during one of our family-night sessions, we read this Chinese fable of the wise peasant:

> Many years ago, a wise peasant lived in China. He had a son who was the apple of his eye. He also was the proud owner of a fine white stallion, which everyone admired. One day his horse escaped from his grounds and disappeared. The villagers came to him one by one and said: "You are such an unlucky man. It is such bad luck that your horse escaped." The peasant responded: "Who knows. Maybe it's bad, maybe it's good." The next day the stallion returned followed by twelve wild horses. The neighbors visited him again and congratulated him on his luck. Again, he just said: "Who knows. Maybe it's good, maybe it's bad."
>
> As it happened, the next day his son was attempting to train one of the wild horses when he fell down and broke his leg. Once more everyone came with their condolences: "It's terrible." Again, he replied: "Who knows. Maybe it's good, maybe it's bad." A few days passed and his poor son was limping around the village with his broken leg, when the emperor's army entered the village announcing that a war was starting and they were enrolling all the young men of the village. However, they left the peasant's son since he had a broken leg. Everyone was extremely jealous of the peasant. They talked about his sheer good luck, while the old man just muttered: "Who knows. Maybe it's good, maybe it's bad."

This fable illustrates that our perception is limited. It is also another reminder that we are not God.

Name Them

The second thing we should remember before beginning our Step Four inventory is that the twelve-step program asks us to be gentle, loving, and kind—even to ourselves. If we can look at ourselves with what psychologist Carl Rogers calls *unconditional positive regard*, in which we accept ourselves for who we are no matter what we find, then Step Four will be one that will help us move towards personal freedom.

I needed to study my character defects and name them. AA's book, *Twelve Steps and Twelve Traditions*, says that character defects are simply our instincts run amok. In nature, those instincts help protect us. Our instincts help us survive by either fighting, fleeing, or freezing in the face of danger. Let's say that there is no apparent danger, but we are afraid that danger may come. If we act on the possibility of danger based on our fears, our instincts become a liability. The idea is to take stock of what we have, assets and defects, and to categorize them. In order to do that, we must closely examine ourselves and our actions.

I had to understand that I was not all bad. I have many positive qualities. I needed to see that because I am a child of God, created in his image and likeness, there was essential good inside me. Otherwise, what would be the use? How could we have any hope? Next, I needed to identify the attitudes and actions that get in the way of my ability to live a fruitful life. Here is where St. Ignatius and the First Principle and Foundation can help us. He reminds us that we are here so that we can praise, reverence, and serve God. And by doing those things, we are saved. Everything that we have and do is to be used to further that Principle. If it helps us to attain that goal, then we should keep it and build upon it. If not, it gets in the way of our recovery, and we should do our best to get rid of it.

It can seem daunting to create a list of the things that we've done wrong. It is important that we remember the requirements of Step Four: to be searching and fearless. I am reminded of a scene from the book *Harry Potter and the Sorcerer's Stone* where Harry was afraid to say the name of his enemy, Voldemort. Dumbledore, his wise teacher, said, "Call him Voldemort, Harry. Always use the proper name for things. Fear of a name increases fear of the thing itself."

People in recovery introduce themselves at AA meetings by their first name, followed by the phrase, "and I'm an alcoholic." If we name our problems, we have brought them out into the light from our subconscious. We stop listening to the deceitful words from the enemy that "we are not enough." And, we take back the control that we lost to fear.

Like an Examination of Conscience prior to receiving the Sacrament of Reconciliation, this inventory is for me alone. It is a gift of awareness. This process allows me to take the time to slow down and examine what has been working for me and what has been getting me into trouble. As I started to dig into the meat of my inventory, I kept reading about my true self and my false self. Perhaps it is the goal of Step Four to uncover my true self.

Remember Adam and Eve in the Garden of Eden? Before they ate of the forbidden fruit, they were naked and free. Once they had eaten and realized their nakedness, they began to cover themselves with fig leaves. Since they'd been naked all along, why would they think that they needed to hide themselves from God? Was pride the "fig leaf" that they used to cover their disobedience?

Are my defects my fig leaves? Why don't I feel that the person God created me to be is enough? Why do I compare myself to others? Where does my shame come from? The goal of my inventory is to help me root out the answers to these questions.

This work is a closer look at my modus operandi (MO). What payoff am I receiving by holding on to character defects or disordered attachments?

I first looked at my dad. It's sometimes easier to be objective about others. He was such a hardworking man, but he never seemed to enjoy the fruits of his labor. One thing that he taught us as kids was the importance of owning land. He was able to achieve his goal.

He owned our home and seventy acres of land. At one time, he also owned twenty-two rental properties.

This focus on work and ownership of land was a constant thread during his lifetime. As I sat down to think about his life in the face of his father's alcoholism, I realized that in his mind, if you could hold down a job and buy your own land (two things that his father never did), you would be stable and safe. If you could do those things, you probably wouldn't become an alcoholic.

But what did he miss in the process? Had these ideas enslaved him in the way that alcohol had enslaved his father?

As I painstakingly went through my list, I began to see some patterns emerge. I could trace most all of my defects to one or two things: fear and shame. Where my father focused on having a job and ownership of land, I had focused on my son's grades. If he got good grades, he'd get into a good college. If he got into a good college, he'd get a good job. And if he got a good job, then he'd be okay. I had inherited this idea unconsciously from my father. It had evolved to add school, but, basically, I was doing what I had learned.

Those *things* meant safety and security. But did they really?

The Meditation on the Two Standards

Ignatian spirituality has another tool to help us with this discernment process. It is called the Meditation on the Two Standards. As a soldier, Ignatius used a lot of examples from the battlefield. A standard is a flag or a banner. One flag is the standard of Christ. The other is the standard of the enemy, or Lucifer, as Ignatius called him.

It seems obvious that we would choose to march under the standard of Christ. But Satan comes in and disguises himself and his true motives. He works in ways that slowly, over time, move us in his direction and away from God. Like the boiled frog, before we know what is happening, we are in over our heads. This meditation asks us to stay vigilant. It helps us to be able to know God and to recognize the enemy.

The enemy, like the world we live in today, strives to be upwardly mobile. The more material possessions he accumulates, the better. Recognition, respect, and applause are important to him. He promotes transactional service. All these things lead us to pride.

Christ chose a simple life. He stayed close to the poor. He lived with little to no recognition. He accepted insults. He aspired to be downwardly mobile. He was truly free. His life teaches us that humility is the doorway to a deeper relationship with God.

One day, as I was reading about the fall of humanity in Genesis, something profound occurred to me. Genesis 2:25 says, "The man and his wife were both naked, and were not ashamed." Then, Genesis 3 begins by introducing the serpent into the Garden. He sets out to cause confusion. Adam and Eve take their focus away from what God promised them and take a bite from the fruit of the tree of knowledge.

As soon as they ate from the tree, four things occurred that had never happened before: Adam and Eve were afraid and they were ashamed. They hid, and they blamed.

I love a good mystery, so when I read those verses again, the timeline jumped out at me. Before Satan, there was no fear or shame. No one hid or blamed.

Since fear and shame were what most of my character defects boiled down to, this process helped me to recognize that those motivations are the calling cards of the enemy. That one realization has helped me to stop myself before I am ruled by my fears or my shame.

At day's end, I often think about the things that God has shown me. Before I began to work these steps, I was afraid of what I might learn about myself. Now, I hear Ignatius's call to look back in order to draw profit, and I am not afraid to look.

WORK THE STEP

Begin by finding a quiet, comfortable spot where you can acknowledge God's presence.

- Read and meditate on Psalm 139.
- Many twelve-step groups sell workbooks solely dedicated to Step Four. I like what the *Big Book* of Alcoholics Anonymous suggests in chapter 5, "How It Works." The suggestion given there helped me get to the heart of my issues, and maybe it will help you too:

  1. Get a notebook and create three columns. The first column is for you to list all of your resentments. The second column is dedicated to the cause of your resentment—why you resent that person, place, or institution. In the third column, identify how that resentment affects you, the fear or shame that your resentment triggers.

  2. Once you've created your list, do you see any patterns emerge?

  3. What fears did those resentments elicit?

  4. Where did those fears originate?

- Read Lamentations 3:39–40. Meditate on why we need to examine our ways. If it helps, write down your thoughts or add details to the list you made earlier.

End this time of personal encounter with God by praying the prayer below or one of your own.

Heavenly Father, it is difficult to search within and list the ways that I have fallen short. I still hear the whispers of the enemy and have the urge to remain hidden. Help me walk through this dark process. Remind me that if I find the things that block the path of our relationship, I will be able to feel your love more deeply. Amen.

STEP FIVE

Coming Clean

Admitted to God, to ourselves, and to another human being the exact nature of our wrongs.
—Step Five of the Twelve Steps

Be grateful for your sins. They are the carriers of grace.
—Anthony de Mello, SJ, *Hearts on Fire: Praying with Jesuits*

My daughter Ellen learned to read a few words at only four years old. Not only could she read these words, but she was also able to write them. She was so thrilled to have these new skills that her writing could be seen on practically every surface in our home. So, my husband and I laid down some boundaries, outlining where she was and wasn't allowed to write.

For a while the choices that we'd given seemed to satisfy her. Then one day, I walked into her closet and saw the name "Olivia" written in pink marker on the wall.

Ellen could not contain her excitement for writing, and so she decided that she would disregard the rules. She thought that if she wrote her sister's name, she would have pulled off the perfect crime. There was only one problem with her plan: her little sister could not yet write her name. I have to admit that it was pretty clever for a four-year-old to figure out that she could point the blame at someone else by writing her name on the wall instead of her own.

We have laughed about that story over the years. But as an adult, I can see in myself the same behaviors that my daughter exhibited at four years old. There are many times when I don't want to accept my limitations.

One such time is when I drive above the speed limit. I begin to rationalize. There isn't much traffic on the highway. It's a clear day for driving. I might blame others—my family made me late, so I need to hurry. I might try to hide my speeding by hitting the brakes if I see a police officer. My actions occur because I am only looking at myself and what I perceive my needs to be. I'm not looking at how this could potentially affect other drivers. I am being self-centered.

If I go deeper still and contemplate exactly what it means to be self-centered, I see that I think I am above the law. I feel that I deserve more than everyone else. I expect others to follow the rules, but they do not apply to me. This feeling of being "above" or "more than" is a dangerous one to have. The reality of this situation is that I have a disordered sense of my place in relationship to God. Since I am relying on myself first, and God as a backup, things can go south rapidly.

Ellen did not come to me that day to confess her wrongdoing; I went to her. She denied knowing anything about the writing on the wall. As a young mother, I'm sure I scolded her. I probably gave her a time-out or took away her markers.

What I didn't see back then was how classic her actions were. This was just another version of the scene in Genesis 3, with different actors. We see it over and over again. Ecclesiastes 1:9 even predicts our pattern of behavior:

What has been is what will be,
    and what has been done is what will be done;
    there is nothing new under the sun.

But at the time, do we recognize what we are doing? Do we understand the implications?

It is important that we remember that God gives each of us free will. When we challenge his will for us, or the boundaries that he has put in place for us, we are in a battle of wills with almighty God. Let's also remember that God's intention with regard to boundaries is to keep us safe. God knows the damage that can be done to our lives when we step outside those lines. The rules he set forth were created out of love.

The History of Our Sin

In the first week of the Spiritual Exercises, Ignatius asks us to look at the history of sin in the world and our own personal history of sin. We take the time to look back as an effort to draw profit. We realize that God asks us to come out of hiding because he loves us and wants us to learn from our actions that have kept us from living out our potential. He wants us to enjoy a close relationship with him.

Steps Four and Five give us an opportunity to slow things down and look for patterns in our behaviors. If we can put fear aside and be observers of our own actions, then, instead of putting up defenses, we may be able to learn something about ourselves. Standing up to the fear and shame will lead us to personal freedom.

I am reminded of something that happened to the talk show host David Letterman. He had been unfaithful to his child's mother, whom he later married. A tabloid got hold of the story and sent him a letter, hoping to extort money from him. If he didn't pay, they would expose him and his affair in their paper. Dave decided that he didn't want to be held hostage, and so he went out ahead of the story and fessed up on his television program in front of the world. As soon as he did that, the story lost its power over him. That is not to say that he didn't have a lot of cleanup work to do at home. But as soon as he exposed the problems to the light, his healing began. That is why confession is so good for the soul.

In the last chapter, I mentioned the four things that occurred once Satan entered the Garden: Adam and Eve felt fear and shame; they hid and blamed. If we can recognize these responses in our own lives and get out in front of them by exposing them to the light in confession to God, ourselves, or another trusted individual, our sins will lose their power over us.

Admitting to the Truth of Our Situation

The day after I dropped our son off at rehab for the first time, I pulled the trash can out and set it under our liquor cabinet. I began pouring out the contents of the bottles into the sink and then dropping them into the trash. I continued this task, one bottle after the next, feeling the anger rise. I'd bought each of those bottles. They were right here in my home, where we would often have a drink before dinner.

My thoughts were filled with blame and shame. I couldn't believe all of the ways that I had been contributing to his problem. Why didn't I see what was going on? When the next bottle was empty, I threw it as hard as I could against the last empty one in the can, breaking the glass.

I guess my fit of rage could be heard in the next room because my husband walked in and asked, "What are you doing?"

"I'm emptying the liquor cabinet before he comes home," I said.

He looked into the cabinet at what remained and said, "Well, don't throw out my good whiskey."

"What?" I asked in disbelief.

"Don't throw out my good whiskey," he said, pointing to his favorite brand.

"Our son is in rehab and your one concern is your good whiskey? If that's the case, then you must be an alcoholic too," I said.

The minute the words slipped out of my mouth, I realized that they were true. I was so worried about our son that it never really occurred to me that my husband had a problem too.

After we took our son to rehab, we had a family education night at the rehab facility, where we discussed all the different kinds of alcoholism. Since my husband was always able to get up and go to work the next day, I didn't see him as an alcoholic. The subtle escalation in the amount that he was drinking had not caught my attention. But his priorities in the face of our family crisis, and my new understanding of alcohol addiction, opened my eyes to the reality that existed in our home.

Deep down inside, I knew things weren't going well. Now, I had to come out of hiding to face the facts. I was the only sober adult in our home. How could I ever share this information with others? How could I keep it to myself and stay sane?

In active addiction, family members recognize that things aren't going well when their loved ones isolate. When we are in hiding, we don't face our problems. We turn a blind eye, hoping that it will all go away. This is denial. Each feeling or intuition we started to pay attention to seemed to bring the true picture of our family into focus.

Father Joseph Martin, a recovering alcoholic and one-time patient at Guest House in Michigan (a recovery center for priests and religious folk), recommends in his famous "Chalk Talks" that we tell all to a safe few. It took a little time, but slowly I began to share my situation with those few trusted friends and family members. They were instrumental in helping me deal with my own personal shame.

I worried about the effect that this problem would have on my addicted loved ones. What would people think of them? Would they be judged unfairly? While I was happy to share my story, I needed to respect the fact that their story belonged to them. I recognize that while their stories are connected to mine, they do not belong to me.

They will need to decide what and with whom they share their stories, because the judgment and lack of understanding that still surrounds this disease is real.

Removing Stigma

Bill Wilson's wife, Lois, understood this shame to be a significant obstacle to opening up with others. She observed in her memoir *Lois Remembers*, "The stigma of alcoholism still is strong. I believe it to be one of the responsibilities of our Fellowships to try to remove this stigma." Yet, stigma, which Oxford Languages defines as a "mark of disgrace" and the singular form of the word stigmata, is probably the main reason that alcoholic families still stay hidden today. Things are slowly improving. We are beginning to see celebrities open up about their addictions. This helps us in starting an honest conversation about what addiction really is. It illustrates that anyone can be touched by this disease. It provides understanding. And I think these conversations are still needed today.

Back in the 1960s and 1970s, alcoholics were comic relief on television. I remember Otis, the town drunk on *The Andy Griffith Show*, and the actors Foster Brooks and Dean Martin, who often played drunks, slurring their words and stumbling about. These shows tended to present an amusing, comical side to alcoholism. If you watch television today, especially a crime drama such as *Law and Order*, you will see and hear the police and others using pejorative language to describe addicts or alcoholics. Their words seem to ignore the fact that part of the disease tells them that they can't live without their substance. Once addicted, the choice is gone. Many scenes show the worst parts of addiction, dehumanizing the one who suffers.

These examples represent two extreme and fictional versions of addiction. They fail to give an accurate representation of the disease.

Few families find alcoholism funny, and most can still see the good within their loved one.

Anyone can suffer from an addiction. Certainly he can be a homeless person, but he can also be a doctor or lawyer. She can be the room mom in your child's classroom. He can be a plumber or even a priest. This disease does not discriminate. And there are varying degrees and types of addictions.

The problem with these stereotypes, besides the obvious negativity directed at those who suffer, is that addicts, alcoholics, and their families will often buy into the hype. Like you and me, addicts and alcoholics have both good and bad qualities. The battle of good versus evil goes on inside of every person. There are no exceptions.

Reading the book *The Anonymous Disciple*, written by Gerard E. Coggins about the life of Father Jim Collins, SJ, I was touched by the hurt and the struggle that Father Collins felt because of his disease. This book gives great insight into the cycle of pain, use, and abuse that those who suffer from addictions face. Here, Father Jim shares about his fifth step with his sponsor, Austin Ripley:

> Some of the old Jesuits were saints. I knew that. I could see it in their faces. They had a quality of goodness, of wisdom, of peace.
>
> Beneath the grandiosity there was that hunger. I wanted to do something worthwhile, something noble. I wanted to touch hearts, to enlighten. I wanted to be a blessing in the lives of others.
>
> What happened?
>
> Pills. Booze. It was all so gradual. I didn't set out to drink. I didn't set out to become addicted to drugs. Pain, pills, booze. Pain, pills, booze. More and more. I forgot about being a blessing in the lives of others. I was simply First-Class Collins.
>
> But there was more to it than that. Deep down, very deep, very far down, I still had the hunger. I still wanted to serve. I still wanted to kiss the leper.
>
> But I couldn't. Booze, pills, and pain.

Father Collins found sobriety. As a result, I imagine that he kissed many a leper. At his funeral, his brother and his fellow Jesuits were shocked when they had to move his service from a small chapel to a bigger church because droves of people showed up to pay their respects to this anonymous disciple.

Step Five says, "Admitted to God, to ourselves, and to another human being the exact nature of our wrongs."

Tell All to a Safe Few

Step Five asks us to admit the exact nature of our wrongs to God first. Many of us have been isolated by fear and shame. This step begins the action of removing us from that isolation and returning us to God, ourselves, and our fellow human beings.

In our Catholic faith, we have the Sacrament of Reconciliation, more commonly known as confession, at our disposal. When speaking of this sacrament, I prefer the term *reconciliation* over the word *confession*. When I hear "confession," I tend to think of a defendant sitting in an interrogation room confessing to a crime. The word *reconciliation* connotes the idea of healing a relationship.

Still, there is nothing more unnerving for a convert than the idea of confession. It's been a long time since this event, but I still remember that we were not ourselves in the RCIA meeting that one night. It was springtime, and we'd grown comfortable with each other since our class had begun in August the previous year. On this night, however, the room was quiet, with only the occasional creaking of wooden floorboards as we moved about the room, looking at various versions of the examination of conscience. It was as if the weight of our worries groaned with each step that we took.

Father Choby, who taught the class, was a kind man. His ample build was as generous as his heart. And when he looked at you, his eyes twinkled as if to suggest that you were his favorite child.

Sensing our worry, Father said, "You can just look over the Ten Commandments and begin your examination of conscience from there, if you'd like."

The room remained quiet. Then Sam, a fellow convert, imagined a softer way of confessing, reminiscent of ordering from a drive-through window menu: "Father, can we just say, I broke two number 4's, three number 2's . . .?"

The room erupted with laughter. His humor released some of the pressure that had been building. We were all adults. Still, we were all clearly rattled at the idea of exposing those parts of ourselves that we were perfectly happy to leave hidden. I guess that is the human condition. They say that confession is good for the soul. And yet, until you get it behind you, the fear and shame can be paralyzing.

A drive-through confession sounded so appealing. Being able to hide behind a number of a commandment I had broken seemed a lot easier than naming my offenses specifically. But it is that humiliation that we each face in it that leads us to humility. Seeing ourselves as someone who has both good and bad traits and accepting the good and bad humbles us. It opens us up to others when we recognize our own imperfections. That vulnerable place is where we will be able to find out who we really are. It takes a lot of courage and prayer to go to that place.

In chapter 6, "Into Action," of the *Big Book* of Alcoholics Anonymous, it says that until you tell another person your entire life story, you don't learn enough about fearlessness, honesty, or humility. And humility is the key to Step Five.

In Step Four, I've taken stock. I've tried to place each item into a category. Is it an asset or is it a defect? And I hold on to those assets. I can build upon the good. I must also strip away the defects, because only then can I uncover what is real about myself. In the search for my true self, I have to learn to weed out the false self. This task can only be completed by figuring out what is given to me by God and what is manufactured by me.

The images that I create are subconsciously intended to cover up who I really am and are motivated by fear and shame. Maybe I've looked about and compared myself to my neighbor. If I feel that he is better, stronger, or smarter than I am, then I may feel the need to puff myself up so that I don't look so small next to him.

The masks that I create help me feel different than the way that my mind sees me. Are these my own, personal fig leaves covering my fears? In my mind, they make me feel like I am more than who God created me to be. There is still an unconscious internal struggle to be the god of my understanding. This created sense of personal identity is what we might call the *ego*.

Twelve-steppers talk a lot about the ego. Some say that Step Five is all about deflating our egos. Some say that *ego* even stands for "edging God out." One friend reminds me that when he is disquieted with himself, he looks to see if his ego is right-sized. The greatest weapon to combat our ego is humility.

Father Ed Dowling, SJ, wrote about this idea in a letter to Bill W., published in the book *The Soul of Sponsorship: The Friendship of Fr. Ed Dowling, SJ, and Bill Wilson in Letters*: "I am sensible, as you are, of God's closeness to human humility. I am sensible, also, of how close human humility can come to humiliation, and I know how close humiliation can come to an alcoholic."

Alcoholics and addicts use alcohol and drugs to cover their feelings of being *less than*. Because they drink, they feel ashamed. Because they feel the shame, they drink. And the cycle continues. Humiliation is a central part of that equation.

It can seem as if our own story will be the worst. We can't imagine anyone as bad as we are. This is the ego trying to keep us silent. Father Fred Harkins, SJ, in *Father Fred and the Twelve Steps*, tells the story of preparing to give his fifth step to his sponsor, Austin Ripley, at Guest House in Michigan.

Just before they met, Father Fred feared that his story would be so shocking that his sponsor might go and sell it to *Life* magazine. Once he sat down with him, Austin stopped him during different points and shared similar stories from his own life. After nine hours of sharing and Austin falling asleep once, Father Fred realized that his story wasn't all that exceptional.

Basically, this step asks us to come out of hiding. My program is quick to remind me, "You are only as sick as your secrets."

Unload the Burden

It turns out that my program seems to know what it's talking about. This quote from Brené Brown's book *Daring Greatly* explains what scientists are learning about the problem of shame.

> Shame thrives on secret keeping, and when it comes to secrets, there's some serious science behind the twelve-step program saying, "You're only as sick as your secrets." In a pioneering study, psychologist and University of Texas professor James Pennebaker and his colleagues studied what happened when trauma survivors—specifically rape and incest survivors—kept their experiences secret. The research team found that the act of not discussing a traumatic event or confiding it to another person could be more damaging than the actual event. Conversely, when people shared their stories and experiences, their physical health improved, their doctor's visits decreased, and they showed significant decreases in their stress hormones.

When I was volunteering for the Homeward Bound program at our county jail, I worked with some of the ladies by holding a twelve-step meeting there once a week. In this particular group, the women became upset at the idea of doing their fourth and fifth steps. Many of these women felt as if every volunteer group that came into the jail wanted to make the focus of their class what they had done wrong, with the intent of teaching them a lesson. The way they saw it, it was easy to know what they'd done wrong; it was another thing altogether to understand why they had done it.

Even though Step Four looks at both our assets and our defects, the women in the county jail had trouble seeing the fourth and fifth steps as anything other than a tool to point out their faults. Instead of working those steps, they wanted to write their stories. Then, they took turns sitting with me one-on-one to share them.

These women had all come from some pretty hard places. I looked for some direction on how to get the greatest benefit from this writing exercise. I used the book written by James W. Pennebaker and John F. Evans, called *Expressive Writing: Words that Heal,* to begin priming the pump. I thought that if we did this exercise before beginning their life stories, it might help them see the benefits of looking back without blame. I wanted them to be able to draw profit from this exercise.

The book asks each person to write about his or her worst trauma for 15–20 minutes a day, five days in a row. This writing is for his or her eyes only. The professors suggest that each writer refrain from worrying about grammar, spelling, or punctuation. Instead, the focus should be on how he or she *felt* during their experience.

After we spent one week on that exercise, we discussed how they felt during the process of writing about their experiences. Most of the girls hated it in the beginning. By the end of the week, there was a shift. They began to see themselves as people who carried a lot of hurt and had survived the best way that they knew how, instead of people who were inherently bad.

For whatever reason, simply getting the secret out—even if it is only on paper—takes away shame's power. The gift of Step Five is this: the effect of shame is lessened; kinship between God and myself and my fellow man is restored. We are helped to know who and what we are, as well as gain an appreciation for who we can be.

To me, that writing exercise felt like a success. It was my hope that they could feel love and mercy towards themselves. Feeling that love, they may be able to look back as a way to learn more about the person that God created them to be. If we can all understand this, it will be easier to come out of hiding.

At least, that is what it took in my case. I had to work my program enough to see that my actions were a method of survival that no longer worked. I remember thinking about the Scripture in Luke 23:34 where Christ is on the cross between the two criminals, and he speaks out, "Father, forgive them; for they do not know what they are doing."

As I grieved the actions that I'd taken towards my addicted loved ones, the second part of that verse, "they know not what they do," began to make sense to me. In the moment we do something wrong, how many of us truly understand the full weight of our actions?

Step Five is key to healing our isolation and loneliness. This step achieves our goal by making us face our humanity. We do this by humbly admitting to God, ourselves, and another human being exactly who we are and what we've done.

Confession doesn't change the facts; it changes the relationships. If I can accept my sinful nature, then I can accept God's forgiveness. Now that my relationship has been rightly ordered, I can accept direction.

Find a Sponsor and/or Spiritual Director

Step Five and Ignatian Spirituality help us to "see with a new pair of glasses," as they say in the meeting rooms. One thing that helps us see differently is connecting with another individual as we go through the process. Twelve-steppers get a sponsor; those who practice Ignatian Spirituality get spiritual direction.

As someone who has both a sponsor and a spiritual director, I can say that both of these roles involve a lot of listening. My sponsor helps me to see myself as I truly am, basing my perspective on the principles of the program. My spiritual director helps me see where God has been in my life. Both help me look for patterns. I feel blessed to have both of these individuals in my life. The help that each gives complements the other.

Father Fred explains in *Father Fred and the Twelve Steps* why having a sponsor is so critical to recovery:

> I need the program, not just part of it, and I need you. I suppose it's a commonplace thing that I become me by sharing with you. I can't do it alone. I can't remain in hiding from God, myself, and my neighbor and hope to grow. It is by coming out of isolation through this Fifth Step and sharing with God, with myself, and another human being, that I come out into the daylight. I need you. It can be a real encounter between real people who are not lying to themselves or to God or to others—people who are seriously and truthfully facing the problem, and honestly with God's help doing something about it.

While my daughter was in grad school in Louisiana, I attended a directed retreat at the Jesuit Spirituality Center in Grand Coteau, Louisiana. It was a particularly difficult time. I was still wrestling with how much help I would give to my son while he was still in active addiction.

My spiritual director visited with me for the first time and mainly listened to me talk. He asked questions and would sometimes share his own experiences with others who'd been affected by the disease. Before I left, he reached up onto his bookshelf and pulled out Henri J. M. Nouwen's *The Return of the Prodigal Son*. He flipped through the pages and found a passage that he marked for me to take with me to read and meditate on.

The passage was hard for me to read. It was so difficult that I had to take it in a little at a time over the weekend. It is the true story that we all face as children, siblings, parents, or loved ones of those affected by this disease.

> God has never pulled back his arms, never withheld his blessing, never stopped considering his son the Beloved One. But the Father couldn't compel his son to stay home. He couldn't force his love on the Beloved. He had to let him go in freedom, even though he knew the pain it would cause both his son and himself. It was love itself that prevented him from keeping his son home at all cost. It was love itself that allowed him to let his son find his own life, even with the risk of losing it.
>
> Here the mystery of my life is unveiled. I am loved so much that I am left free to leave home. The blessing is there from the beginning. I have left it and keep on leaving it. But the Father is always looking for me with outstretched arms to receive me back and whisper again in my ear: "You are my Beloved, on you my favor rests."

Step Five and Ignatian spirituality allowed me to confront my guilt and shame. They allowed me to seek the help of others. With the gentle guidance of my director, I was able to finally let go of my son and his disease. I was no longer alone. Now, I was in a right relationship with God and others.

Many people say that in this program we only really do three things: trust God, clean house, and help others. Step Five is where we begin to take action.

WORK THE STEP

Begin by finding a quiet, comfortable spot where you can acknowledge God's presence.

- Read and meditate on Psalm 32.
- If you were to imagine God describing you to someone else, what do you think he would say?
- When you read your response to the question above, did you describe God's response as judgmental or merciful?
- Make a list of qualities you would like to have in either a sponsor or a spiritual director.
- Does the word *humility* have a positive or negative connotation for you? Why?
- Read Ephesians 5:10–17. Notice why we are to bring things into the light.

End this time of personal encounter with God by praying the prayer below or one of your own.

Heavenly Father, I am sorry for the places where I've fallen short. I grieve some of the choices that I have made. I come to you, filled with hope that, with your help, I can repair the bond that was once lost. Thank you for giving me the courage I need to do this task. Amen.

STEP SIX

Entirely Ready

Were entirely ready to have God remove all of these defects
of character.
—Step Six of the Twelve Steps

When taking the first steps on the road of virtue the old man must
be mortified, but in such a way as not to slay the new man.
—St. Ignatius of Loyola

My daughter had a dark bay pony named Casey. He was a marvel. At only thirteen hands, or four feet and four inches, tall (from the ground to the highest point of his withers), he could jump out over the Dutch door of his stall without a running start. This resulted in his being moved to another part of the barn—to a stall that did not have a Dutch door leading outside.

His pony behaviors were more challenging than those of any of the other horses that we'd had up to that point. Some people believe that ponies cause so many problems because they are unusually smart, and I would agree with that assessment.

When we got Casey, it was apparent that a man had probably mistreated him. This was evidenced by his utter refusal to let my husband lead him inside. I could catch him in the field, he would flock to the children as soon as he spotted them in the yard beside his pasture, but if my husband walked outside with a halter in hand, Casey looked like a miniature racehorse out for a sprint.

We understood that he would need to establish trust with us and that it would take many trips into the barn at night for him to accept that going inside was a good thing. Time and routine would establish that if he came to his owner, then his stall awaited him. In it, new bedding would be added, clean water would fill his bucket, and fresh-cut grass hay and just the right amount of sweet feed would be in his feeder. His herd would all be tucked inside munching on their hay. He could join them, out of the reach of night-prowling coyotes and foxes who searched for animals they could overtake. In his stall, he would be fed and protected, and he could lie down and rest.

So, why did he run? Why did he lap the field over and over again? Why would he sometimes approach the gate, running near my husband, Matt, then turn his butt at the last minute, striking out with both back feet as if saying, "I'll get you before you get me"? This man he kicked at was the very person who cleaned his stall, filled his water bucket, and dumped hay and grain into his feeder each day. He was the one who provided him with health, protection, and comfort.

After a while, we noticed that this kind of performance occurred when my husband was in a hurry. If he was rushed and not relaxed, Casey would start to get antsy. Then my husband would grow frustrated. As soon as Casey sensed his frustration, he would take flight.

You see, Casey could not forget the man who was unkind. While my husband was not the one who mistreated him, he triggered that memory for Casey. His fear was too great for him to remember whom he belonged to now.

My husband has owned horses his whole life. So, after we had Casey for a while, and he had time to know and trust us, my husband changed tactics. He knew that if he ran after Casey, Casey would only run harder. He would become more and more afraid; his adrenaline would kick in. It would be a real battle of the wills. Instead, when Casey approached the gate, my husband raised both of his hands in the air and began waving them at Casey, yelling for him to move away from the gate.

The first time I saw my husband do this, I thought that he was crazy.

"What are you doing?" I asked.

"I'm giving him what he wants," he said.

"How's that?" I asked.

"He wants to run. I'm allowing him to do it. If he gets tired enough, he will come," he responded.

Matt was giving him his will. He was allowing Casey to respond the way that he needed to when he was afraid. Matt was giving him the time and space to experience how living out his own will would work out for him. It reminds me of the phrase "Be careful what you wish for; you might just get it."

There were a couple of times when Casey slowed down at the gate, and my husband waved his arms and yelled, "Haw! Haw!" so the pony kept running. After a while, it was apparent that he was growing tired from all of that running. That's when he came up to my husband and dropped his head for him to put the halter on; he surrendered.

It was a great lesson, one that I will never forget. It wasn't until I began doing the twelve-step work that I was able to connect the dots.

Step Six seemed so insignificant on first take. Why did I need to be entirely ready for God to remove the things I listed, which end up making me feel bad? These defects of character or inordinate attachments had kept me running around the perimeter of my life, going nowhere. They were my attempt at staying safe. They had become the bars of my own personal prison.

I never understood the meat of this step until I remembered that horse. I was sitting on the sofa trying to figure out how to use this step in my life when, out of the blue, this memory of Casey and my husband coming to an understanding flooded my thoughts. Then it seemed perfectly clear.

Step Six says, "Were entirely ready to have God remove all these defects of character."

Get to the Root of the Problem

Being "entirely ready" means, first and foremost, that I have surrendered my will. Step Six is very much like Step Three, except this time I used it to turn inward. In Step Three, I surrendered control of my son and my husband to the will of God. For those who suffer from addiction, they give up their mind-altering substance. We all start in Step Three with the clear and present danger that exists in our own lives, whatever that may be. We must remember that their drinking or drug use and our need to control are only symptoms of our deeper problems.

Step Six asks us to focus on the root of our problems. This is a very big job. The changes don't occur in an instant. And we can't go through this process alone. It takes a lifetime of work in cooperation with God. Father Ed Dowling speaks to this:

> I think the sixth step is the one which divides the men from the boys in AA. It is a love of the cross. The sixth step says that one is not almost, but entirely ready, not merely willing, but ready. The difference is between wanting and willing to have God remove all these defects of character. You have here, if you look into it, not the willingness of Simon Cyrene to suffer but the great desire or love, similar to what Chesterton calls Christ's love affair with the cross. ("Catholic Asceticism and the Twelve Steps", NCCA Blue Book, 1953)

Since I let go of my control over my loved ones in Step Three, the sixth step is an opportunity to look at the things within me that will either stand in my way or help me grow my relationships with God and others.

My relationship with my son required change. Old habits die hard, but my mode of relating to him and others could not remain as it was and be healthy. I would need to check myself and keep the focus on me. I needed to ask myself, *What things did I do that contributed to our problems?*

Like my stubborn pony, it only took a small thing to trigger an old memory. If my son did one thing that was reminiscent to me of his days in active addiction, fear kicked in. For me, that meant that I became angry and unreasonable. I often started trying to control something that he was doing. Yet, if I let go of these defense mechanisms, how can I be sure that I will be safe? Shouldn't I send a clear message about what is right and what is wrong? If I drop these controlling habits, will that make it appear that I agree with whatever he is doing? Will it make me a negligent parent?

Step Six is like those last few laps around the field. I'm getting tired, I'm exhausted from the fear and anxiety, but am I tired enough? Am I entirely ready to trust these things to God?

This step peels back another layer of control. It exposes the struggle for what it is. It is a battle of the wills. I still want to take a stab at playing God, but this twelve-step program is literally giving me the baby steps that I need for maintaining healthy relationships. In William Barry's *Lenten Meditations: Growing in Friendship with God*, he observes this battle:

> The lie at the heart of human sinfulness is that we gain control of our existence by some action of our own and that God does not want us to have this power. God creating human beings in God's own likeness is described in the first creation account in Genesis. But instead of accepting friendship with God that was offered,

human beings chose to enter into rivalry with God. The consequences of that disastrous choice plague our world still.

As in Step Three, we need to use those three A's (Awareness, Acceptance, and Action) to work Step Six. Father Barry's take on our human condition illuminates that we have a choice. We can either compete with God for control or we can enter into a friendship with him and participate in his plan for our lives. Do we realize what it is that we are doing? Can we slow things down enough to become aware of what is actually at play?

In Step Six we move beyond treating the symptoms and work towards healing the disease instead. We began the process in Steps One through Three by first recognizing our powerlessness, realizing that God is the one who holds the power, and then handing it (our illusion of control) over to him. We are restoring order between ourselves and God, in keeping with the First Principle and Foundation of St. Ignatius's Spiritual Exercises. We move on to the work that is needed within ourselves (Step Four). We begin by taking inventory of our defects. Next, we let those secrets out into the light by sharing them with God, ourselves, and another trusted individual (Step Five).

Now that we are entirely ready for God to work, it will be helpful to understand a little more about those character defects that we've listed and shared. Why would we ever want to hold on to something that is a defect? Why would we attach to something that is inordinate or defined as excessive? In *Father Fred and the Twelve Steps*, Father Fred writes, "There are some defects, some second-rate ways of facing reality, that I have, that are so familiar to me and that I rely on so much, that I'm afraid to let go of them."

Scripture addresses this problem in Romans 7:14–17, saying, "For we know that the law is spiritual; but I am of the flesh, sold into slavery under sin. I do not understand my own actions. For I do not do what I want, but I do the very thing I hate. Now if I do what I do not want, I agree that the law is good. But in fact it is no longer I that do it, but sin that dwells within me."

Ignatian spirituality uses the terms *detachment* or *indifference* when we seek to rid ourselves of the things that get in the way of our relationship with God. Oddly enough, the recovery community uses the same language—"detachment with love"—to separate ourselves from the chaos of the disease of addiction. We detach from the disease and not the person, so our program adds the qualification "with love" to the word *detachment*. Thus, we detach with love. It is important to realize that the choice we make in letting go is done with love instead of with anger that we feel towards the disease of addiction. Still, it takes a lot of courage to detach, whether it be from our addicted loved ones or from our old habits.

Offer Yourself Mercy

If I am to remove these traits, with God's help, wouldn't it be easier to do by understanding what payoff I get from them? If I can gain awareness of whatever unconscious reason I have for using these traits, then will I be able to see how ineffective, even harmful, they have become?

I am reminded of how transformative our awareness can be by something that happened quite accidentally one semester during the Homeward Bound program at the county jail. This was the largest class that I'd had up to that point, and over half of the women had experienced things that I really knew nothing about. During our initial meeting, several women shared that they had been victims of either sexual violence, exploitation, or trafficking.

Let's face it, I was only a middle-class, middle-aged volunteer who didn't have any experience with this kind of trauma. I felt overwhelmed and unqualified to teach these women anything about anything. How could I understand what they had been through? I began to complain to God a bit. Why would he put me in this situation? I was clearly in over my head. What could I offer, when these women needed a professional? What was he thinking?

After I got some whining out of my system, I sat down at my computer and did a bit of Googling. My thought was, *If you aren't an expert, consult one.* I decided to look for a little bibliotherapy and found a book that I thought might be just perfect for these ladies. It addressed the sexual trauma experienced by a young girl and was written by a woman who had taught writing to homeless and at-risk youth throughout Los Angeles for more than sixteen years. I decided that this semester we'd have a book club, and Cynthia Bond's book, *Ruby*, would be our selection.

I ordered the books and proudly brought them to class. As I handed out each crisp, new book to the women, I saw them each sit a little straighter; smiles replaced vacant stares, and hands began to caress their book like it was a fragile treasure. They'd never been in a book club before.

Maybe God knew what he was doing . . . I was so pleased. I assigned the first few chapters and told the women that I was as excited as they were to read and discuss those chapters the next week. I left feeling on top of the world.

It didn't take long to get over that feeling. You see, this story is about the sexual exploitation and slavery that this young girl, Ruby, endured. The descriptions were graphic and horrifying. In the book, the words spoken to a child by a grown man, whose sole intention was to objectify her, were beyond what I could have imagined. The writer's words haunted me long after I laid the book down.

My intention was to do something good for these women, and now I had probably stirred up some terribly bad memories. What was I thinking? I felt like a fool for entertaining the idea that I could actually help. The dialogue in this book was sickening to me. What's more, the jail has some pretty strict rules about what is brought inside. Had I brought pornography to these women?

The next week when I arrived back at the class, sullen expressions met me at the door. "I don't like this book, Miss Jean," one of the women said.

"Do we have to keep reading?" asked another.

I'd been praying about what to do, and the feeling I got was that we should keep reading. The writer works with at-risk youth. Surely, the material that she produced would not be written with the intention of harming them. So, I asked them to trust me and keep going. And I held my breath.

Week after week, we trudged through that story, and then I saw something begin to happen that helped me see what I never would have considered had we not traveled this journey together.

In the story, Ruby was badly abused, and in the process, lost her sense of self and even her mind. *Surely some redeeming thing is going to happen*, I kept thinking. Maybe a knight in shining armor will show up to rescue her. But, as it is in life, one never came. Instead, one young man loved her. His love for her was pure and selfless. He kept showing up, asking nothing from her, and over time, she was able to accept his love. Bit by bit, that love filled her up enough that she was able to both love and save herself.

Like the Twelve Steps, this book shows that we can only change ourselves. It is an empowering story, but the unexpected gift was what the book exposed to the women in my class. These women probably had heard similar things said to them; they might have suffered some of the same experiences that this young girl had. Except now they were seeing those things happen to an innocent child. They saw that she wasn't a flawed individual or that she deserved the treatment she received. If they could accept that about Ruby, then maybe they could see the same truth in their own situation. Perhaps, they could offer the same mercy to themselves.

That intense book was able to help these ladies become aware that *what happened to them* was not because of *who they are*. Their shame was holding them hostage. It made them afraid to come out of hiding.

We all feel, at various times and in different situations, that we don't fit in or measure up. Shame and guilt are the culprits for this feeling. We are afraid of being exposed. AA's book *Twelve Steps and Twelve Traditions* says, "The chief activator of our defects has been self-centered fear—primarily fear that we would lose something we already possessed or would fail to get something we demanded." My program says that *fear* stands for "False Evidence Appearing Real." These statements gave me hope from the beginning.

As I continued to learn, I kept coming back to the passage in Genesis 3 regarding the fall of Adam and Eve. Fear and shame are always popping up. So, it's important to take a closer look at what they are.

The writer Ernest Kurtz created a little booklet called *Shame & Guilt*, taken from a paper he wrote for professionals and then simplified. I printed it off in the hopes that I could figure out the link between my character defects and shame. His work is not easy reading, but as I waded through the text, I learned some very important things about shame.

Kurtz states that for every human being there are two distinct ways of feeling bad: guilt and shame. He says, "The impressive success of Alcoholics Anonymous in dealing with alcoholism and addiction flows directly from A.A.'s effectiveness with healing shame."

He feels that it is very important that we learn the difference between the two words *guilt* and *shame*. This is important because each requires a different mode of healing. Guilt comes from violating a boundary. Shame tells us that we don't measure up. Guilt is about something we did; shame is about who we are. Kurtz believes that shame associates itself with "being caught," which then leads to a mixed-up relationship with guilt. As I began to understand a bit about shame and guilt, it seemed that I saw them confused everywhere.

The women in my class needed to become aware of the fact that they are children of God, made in his image. While they needed to see this truth, it was also necessary for them to accept it. When we feel unworthy, it may require a lot of time and healing to accept that we are enough in God's eyes, even though we are human and *all* fall short.

Ruby helped to bring a child's shame out into the light. The writer was able to tell the story in such a way that it exposed shame for the deception that it really is. The women in my class were able to see that too.

That semester is one that I will never forget. I often felt like I was walking in the dark. In the end, I think we all healed some. The women could see themselves a little more clearly, and I learned a lot about God's healing love for us.

As I worked on Step Six, I learned that our character defects are primarily our defense mechanisms. Somewhere along the way, our pride, anger, resentments, fear, self-pity, lying, impatience, and perfectionism—to name just a few—are the shields or swords we use to keep ourselves and others from seeing something that we fear more than anything else: that we are not enough.

In the earlier class that I taught on Moral Reconation Therapy, the women and I learned that what we believe informs our attitudes and that our attitudes influence our behavior. I used that information to question my view of God. Understanding that I needed to observe my own beliefs about God, in order to understand my attitudes and behaviors, helped me get to the root of why I was keeping God at a distance. The image of God that I held in my mind was not based on trust, and it also was not accurate.

Now, I needed to take that same formula and look at myself. *What do I really believe to be true about myself? Who am I in reality? Has my perception been skewed?* And, *Where have I felt shame in my life?*

This exercise reminds me of a segment that I saw on the *Today Show*, in which an artist drew an image based on a description that a person gave of himself or herself. Then, that person's friend gave a description. The artist worked with about twenty different people and their friends. Without fail, the portraits done based on the friend's description were always closer to the actual image of the person.

Similarly, what lies about myself have I been living with? Won't it be a relief to see that I am not less than human? Since I'm compensating for self-degrading ideas that I hold for myself, won't I be more at ease if I can stop trying to be more than human?

Step Six can help us find answers to these questions. If we can let go of our will, which seeks to protect something that isn't true, then we will find relief. Oxford Language's dictionary definition of *reality* is "The world or the state of things as they actually exist, as opposed to an idealistic or notional idea of them." By the time I'd worked this step, I was beginning to get an accurate picture of my life. My views of God and of self (and the relationship between the two) were beginning to take on new meaning.

WORK THE STEP

Begin by finding a quiet, comfortable spot where you can acknowledge God's presence.

- Read and meditate on Psalm 9.
- What character defects from Step Five get you in trouble most of the time?
- Being as honest as you can, how would you describe yourself to a stranger?
- How does that description align with the fact that you were made in God's image and likeness?
- Read Matthew 11:28–30. Notice what Jesus offers us.

End this time of personal encounter with God by praying the prayer below or one of your own.

Heavenly Father, help me to notice when I stubbornly resist accepting your will. Give me the courage to trust you and let go of my old habits and defense mechanisms. Help me to remember those times when I have let go and found that things have gone better than I could have ever imagined. I need you close so that I can remember that your will is always what is best for me. Thank you for loving me despite my resistance. Amen.

STEP SEVEN

Humility

Humbly asked Him to remove our shortcomings.
—Step Seven of the Twelve Steps

The centurion answered, "Lord, I am not worthy to have you come under my roof; but only speak the word, and my servant will be healed."
—Matthew 8:8

I recently watched the show "Off Camera—with Sam Jones," featuring an interview with the actor Dax Shepherd. The host, Sam Jones, was interested in discussing an incident that occurred when radio personality Gordan Keith was at Dax's house and stumbled upon his copy of the book *Alcoholics Anonymous*.

Gordan opened the front cover of his friend's *Big Book* and noticed that there was a long list of dates, all crossed out with the exception of the last one. Next to each crossed-out date was a negative comment.

Curious, and sensing the personal nature of what he'd found, Gordan decided to go to Dax to fess up to what he'd done and to ask his friend what it meant. Realizing which page his friend had seen, Dax was humiliated. He felt embarrassed that he had been powerless over drugs and alcohol for so long. Nevertheless, he explained that each marked-through date represented a time when he had tried to quit using drugs and drinking alcohol but was unsuccessful. Frustrated with his inability to quit, he wrote himself a self-deprecating note beside each entry. The last date on the list was the one when he was finally able to find and maintain his sobriety.

While looking at the same book and the same page that brought so much shame to Dax, Gordan's focus was on something totally different. Gordan had faced his own struggles with addiction, and what he saw on that page was someone who did not quit quitting. He saw someone who didn't die. He found hope in Dax's persistence to find sobriety; Dax never gave up and eventually found success.

Dax was then able to notice how emotional Gordan was about his dogged determination, and suddenly his perception shifted. Without shame, Dax was able to accept his failures as an inspiration of hope for his friend. This situation offered the clarity needed to see himself as he truly was. But why had Dax struggled to see beyond his failed attempts at sobriety? And why is it so difficult to see ourselves as others may see us?

Step Seven begins with the word *humbly*. The Alcoholics Anonymous book *Twelve Steps and Twelve Traditions* says, "For those who have made progress in A.A., [humility] amounts to a clear recognition of what and who we really are, followed by a sincere attempt to become what we could be."

What Are My Filters?

As I try to understand this idea of humility, I am reminded of the use of filters on Instagram. As a child of the 70s and 80s, I didn't take selfies. I find this new practice quite interesting as I observe young people staring into their phones while taking snapshots of themselves. Then they will consciously choose to change their appearance by applying a filter on top of that image. This change in appearance can be complimentary, or it can be funny and playful. Sometimes, people will distort the image of themselves or others in a negative way.

Whatever the case, these filters change the original image of the person in the photo.

This analogy helps me understand humility. I associate humility with that original photo. It is what you see in reality. Perhaps the reason we can't see things so clearly is because we each unconsciously filter everything through our own experiences. Sometimes our experience creates a filter of fear.

Imagine observing everything in our environment while searching for the ways in which it can hurt us. Maybe life has created a filter of resentment. Something has happened to us before and we know it can happen to us again. We can't let it go. Could it be that we have created a self-centered filter because if we don't stand up for ourselves, we know that no one else will? Our created filters make our vision one-sided. So, what do these filters mean? And what can we do to eliminate them? If we look closely at each of our filters, then we may find two ways of seeing ourselves that are two sides of the same coin: shame and pride.

Shame and Pride

Dax's story highlights some of shame's great lies: "You are a failure." "You should be able to do this alone." "No one else will understand." Let's remember Ernst Kurtz's words in *Shame & Guilt*: "The impressive success of Alcoholics Anonymous in dealing with alcoholism and addiction flows directly from A.A.'s effectiveness with healing shame." He goes on to say that AA confronts shame right off the bat in Step One, when we are forced to admit our powerlessness. Every person must become aware and accept that he or she is powerless over alcohol or whatever addiction he or she faces. Once people have "outed" themselves, shame loses its power.

Pride can also become excessive. Where shame says you are not enough, pride says you are more than enough; you are the best. Pride is still a tool of the shame-filled to hide their feelings of inadequacy. Pride is like a fancy dress, worn to cover up the feelings of insufficiency of the shame-filled.

As I began to think about seeing my life as it actually was and is, I imagined a game of tug-of-war: pride and shame always pulling at me from either side. I must remember to maintain a stance away from either of those extremes.

Balance and Self-Deception

Step Seven says, "Humbly asked Him to remove our shortcomings."

Saint Ignatius was aware of another obstacle that people face in seeking the truth about themselves. The American writer Richard Bach made this idea well-known when he said, "The worst lies are the lies that we tell ourselves." Ignatius understood his own tendency to temper the truth so that it was something he could live with. He knew that humility was essential, and he also knew that when things get difficult, we often try to wiggle our way out of the hard places. So, he came up with two exercises to help us foresee those problems so that we could be perfectly conscious of the choices that we are making.

The first exercise is the Meditation on the Two Standards that I mentioned back in chapter 4. It serves to teach us about Jesus and to help us uncover our natural human tendency towards self-deception by making us aware of the *culture* that leads to self-deception. Socially, we are born into a certain common sense that we unknowingly buy into. We need to become aware of our values and narratives. For example, in the US, fame, power, and privilege are regarded as values that we should work towards, even though those values run counter to the values of Christ. We are asked to notice this discrepancy in the Meditation on the Two Standards exercise. Through it, we can begin to discern what is society's influence in our life as opposed to or different from the direction Jesus wants us to go.

The second exercise regarding self-deception is called the Three Types of Person or Three Ways of Saying Yes. This exercise asks us how our *personal psychology* can lead us to self-deception. This can be illustrated in the way that we answer Christ's call to radical discipleship. How open are we to the call of Christ?

To illustrate this exercise, I will give you the example of an alcoholic deciding to quit drinking. The first way of saying yes is by saying, "Yes, I'll quit drinking, tomorrow." (Yes, but . . .) The second way of saying yes is by saying, "Yes, I'll quit drinking whiskey and drink wine instead." (Yes, with wiggle room.) The third way of saying yes is to just say "Yes." (Yes, without condition.)

Humility is something that we must work towards if we are to see the full picture. Not only is it important in our individual lives: it is also important to the lives of our family members.

In his book *Making Choices in Christ: The Foundations of Ignatian Spirituality* Joseph A. Tetlow, SJ, says that "Christian humility, properly understood, requires a strong sense of self, and the greater the humility, the stronger the sense of self. For as more than one saint has remarked, humility is seeing and acknowledging the truth about yourself and your world."

A Strong Sense of Self

"Who is Jean Heaton?" a friend asked me. "Tell me about her." I wasn't sure I could. She asked me to try and remember that girl, who I was growing up. What was she like? What things sparked her curiosity? It was a lot to think about. Then, one day, I remembered. I was running an errand to get horse feed. The feed store was in a small town about twenty miles away. Just before I rounded a sharp curve, I glanced over at the hills that surrounded the valley. It was spring, and the leaves had not yet come out on the trees, which made it easier to see just how steep the hill actually was. Noticing that hill triggered a memory. I remember seeing a similar hill when I was a child out with my dad. I begged him to climb that "mountain" with me. He laughed and said, "We will one day, Sis." But we never took the time.

I drove on down the road, smiling from the memory, and picked up the feed. I realized that the joy of that time in my life was something that I craved. I couldn't get the idea of fulfilling a childhood wish out of my mind. By the time I got home, I had decided to return to the hill to climb it. I could almost feel my program friends cheering me on. I needed to honor the feelings of "want" that God was giving me. Why did I feel this need? What purpose did it serve? And was I nuts for thinking about this adventure in my late forties?

When I got home and unloaded the feed, my daughter Ellen met me at the barn. I looked at her and asked, "Do you want to go on an adventure with me?"

"What?!" she asked.

You see, we didn't have adventures in our home. We rarely had fun. We either worked nonstop or sat around fretting over things beyond our control. I am sure she had a hard time believing that I would even consider having fun or going on an adventure, for that matter.

"Yes, an adventure," I said.

"What kind of adventure?" she asked.

"Well, I just saw this delightful hill on the way home, and I'd love to go with you to climb it."

"Do you know whose property it is?" she asked.

"Oh, it will be fine. It's out in the middle of nowhere," I replied.

"We could be arrested . . . or shot," she said worriedly.

"Now, that would make for a better story, wouldn't it?" I said.

"I'm not kidding, Mom."

"Me either. Go if you want, stay if you want. I'm going in to change into my muck boots."

"Wait up—someone needs to go with you . . . in case the police show up," she called.

My daughter's reactions were the direct result of living in our oh-so-serious household. When addiction moved in, and if I am being honest, well before addiction moved in, joy had left the vicinity. It was evident that it was time to try and salvage the time we had with them while they still lived at home. We needed to put God back at the center of our lives to help us out of the chaos that we'd created.

We got in the car, and I glanced over at my daughter. I could tell that she wanted to be excited. But she was guarded. I understood why. It made me feel sad but determined. She looked great but not exactly ready for a hill climb. Her hair was curled. Her make-up was just right. Even her nails had been freshly polished with glittery purple nail polish. "Do you want to go change into something that you don't mind getting dirty?" I asked.

"I'm sure I'll be fine," she said.

Off we went. Ellen mumbled on about hunters and property owners. "Look up. Isn't this beautiful?" I asked. "Look at the creek at the bottom of the hill. Listen to the water rushing over the rocks. And, look over there!" I said, pointing to the daffodils popping up as far as the eye could see.

We started to climb and saw that the hill was fairly steep. It was so steep, in fact, that we had to grab hold of a nearby branch from a tree to pull ourselves up to the next level.

Last year's leaves made for slippery footing, and before I knew it, I slipped and began to roll back down towards the bottom. "Mom, are you okay?" I could hear as I rolled.

I stopped myself by reaching out to catch the trunk of a small tree and landed on my back with the sunshine warming my face and springtime air filling my lungs. This was the most alive I'd felt in too long to remember.

"I'm fine!" I yelled up to her.

And then, she started laughing. For a while, we hadn't laughed in our home. We just didn't laugh anymore. We'd been stuck on this hamster wheel of worry. But today we were making a change, and I realized that her laughter was one of the loveliest sounds that I'd ever heard. *This*, I thought, *this is what I want for my children.*

Ellen was beginning to have a little fun at my expense. There were a few barbs about my age thrown out there. But our Lord has the sweetest sense of humor, because just as she started to crack another joke, she stepped on a patch of wet leaves that took one leg out from under her, sending her rolling like a log, gaining speed until she was able to stop herself by catching a tree branch.

I made my way towards her, hoping to help get her upright on the steep incline. When I got there, the first thing that I saw were the purple glitter-filled nails dug into the muddy hillside, and I got tickled at the absurdity of it all. It's a lot like our life today. We can be in a difficult season, but it doesn't mean that we should refuse the joy that exists right alongside the hardships. Humility is accepting the existence of the yin and the yang of our situations. We can have joy and pain at the same time. Humility keeps us from being defined by either extreme. Instead, it helps us respond to life knowing that we are not alone.

The sight of those perfectly painted nails, clutching the dark composting leaves and mud, did me in. You could hear the laughter echo across the hills, and tears stained my cheeks. It was as if all the saved-up nervous energy had found a way to escape, and there was no way for it to stop.

Ellen sat up, looked at me, and said, "Thanks, Mom. Gee, thanks. I come to make sure you don't get shot or arrested while having your midlife crisis, and all you do is laugh."

Seeing her covered in mud, attempting seriousness, only made me laugh harder. I was full of joy. My cup ranneth over. All I could think of was, *Thank you, God. Thank you. You are so good to me.*

I will never forget that day. I allowed myself to listen to my feelings, to recognize who I truly was. This freed me to experience joy. When I honor those feelings of want, I move some of my focus off the difficulties we are facing as a family. This begins the work of repairing the image that I hold of myself. Once I regain connection as a child of God, knowing that I was made in his likeness and image, I begin to heal.

We Have a Choice

We get to choose how we spend our time. Things may not be going well, but should we break out a black veil and mourn our life just because things aren't going as we'd hoped? Can we sit still and ask God what we can or should do instead? Shouldn't we take advantage of the good that can temper or balance the other things that are going on in our lives?

A program friend, whom I'll call Donna, illustrates this point each time we have a newcomer in the rooms. She tells the story of why she visited a twelve-step meeting for the first time. Even though Donna was an adult and had already moved out of her parents' home, she was still trying to manage things for her family. Due to his alcoholism, her father had just lost his job and their home, which was part of his salary package. The family had been told that they had to be out of the house that she'd grown up in by June 30 of that year. When she walked in the door of the meeting room with a notebook in hand, she intended to collect the names of the right doctors and lawyers she needed to have her father committed. That was all that she wanted from the meeting. Somehow, she had it in her mind that if she got him committed, even if it was against his will, things would get better in her parents' home.

A wise woman who'd been in the rooms for some time listened to her request and said, "Suppose you collect the names and numbers of those doctors and lawyers, and you make the necessary appointments. And suppose you are able to get your father to attend all of those appointments. Will June 30 still come?"

"Why, of course," Donna answered, a little confused.

"Well, what if instead of getting the numbers, making appointments, taking family members to the appointments that they may or may not be willing to make, you come to meetings? What if you learn about the disease and learn to take care of yourself? Suppose you lean on friends who have been through this before. Will June 30 still come?" she asked.

"Yes. Yes, it will," Donna said.

"June 30 is going to come no matter what. How do you want to feel when it does?" the woman asked.

Humor and Gratitude

Facing our realities can seem impossible at times. But there are a couple of things that both the program and Ernst Kurtz recommend to help us deal with the shame that is at the heart of all of our problems. The first is gratitude.

Early in my days in the program, I was told that if things aren't going the way that I think they should, then I should make a gratitude list. Gratitude keeps resentment from developing. Gratitude helps us see that we aren't entitled to anything in this world. Everything that we have has been given to us. If we make note of the good, then we can maintain our focus and balance. Gratitude keeps us from putting ourselves at the center.

The second tool is humor. The first time we went to family night at our son's rehab center, we were told that his AA group was next door having their meeting; once their meeting was over, their group would join us for the last session. During that first hour, family members were learning a lot of new information about the harsh realities of this disease, and our loved ones next door would break out in laughter. It sounded as if they were having the time of their lives. In our room, parents and spouses were solemn and sad, and tears frequently flowed, but their laughter continued. We would hear an outburst and look at one another. After a while, one parent said, "Well, I wish that we were able to have such a good time."

Now that I've been involved in my program for some time, I can report that once we've had a few meetings under our belts, we, too, laugh often. As I began to research these topics, I learned that laughter is literally good medicine. In practical terms, as loved ones of those who suffer from this disease, it is imperative that we are able to see ourselves in a true light and be able to laugh at ourselves. Remember when I took pictures of the hookahs and bongs in the gas station, in order to wage war against convenience stores that sold paraphernalia? Well, I needed to see how silly that really was.

Sometimes we get so mired in the *crazy* of the disease that we forget to look up and see what we really look like. This is usually why you hear alcoholics laughing during their meetings. They look at the incongruous nature of their actions and stop taking themselves so seriously.

A friend, whom I will call Mary, often shares about a time when her son was in and out of trouble. It was imperative for him to make it to school every day if he was ever to graduate. One morning, he was dragging his feet getting ready and he missed the bus. Mary was worried sick and determined that he would go to school and graduate. So, she got him into her car and chased the school bus down the road, honking and yelling. When the bus pulled over, she got out of her car to tell them that her son needed to be on that bus. It was then that she realized she only had on a bathrobe! It is a great story, and we all laugh each time she tells it, because we have all found ourselves in insane situations before. Our laughter says that there is no expectation of perfection and that it's okay to be human.

The final section of Step Seven is about asking for help in removing our shortcomings. Recognition that we can't do this work alone suggests that we have a certain degree of humility. Asking is also important because God will never force us to do anything. He will wait patiently for us to ask. That is another way that we can see the depth of his love for us.

The work of the sixth and seventh steps prepares us for God's forgiveness. It also starts bringing the root of our problems to our awareness. Let me leave you with AA's Step Seven prayer:

> My Creator, I am now willing that you should have all of me, good and bad. I pray that you now remove from me every single defect of character which stands in the way of my usefulness to you and my fellows. Grant me strength, as I go out from here, to do your bidding. Amen.

WORK THE STEP

Begin by finding a quiet, comfortable spot where you can acknowledge God's presence.

- Read and meditate on Psalm 131.
- Have you prayed for God to make your shortcomings visible to you and remove them?
- In what ways have you lacked humility?
- What masks of pride have you worn to cover your shame?
- What changes can you make that will bring balance to your life?
- Make a gratitude list for today.
- Read Isaiah 41:10 and Exodus 14:14. Notice how God responds when we seek his help.
- What can you learn about God from these verses?

End this time of personal encounter with God by praying the prayer below or one of your own.

Heavenly Father, I want to remove the obstacles that keep me from finding humility, but I am afraid. In my mind, they have kept me safe. I know that I need your help. Please grant me the courage and peace to work with your grace to replace them with something that aligns with your will. Thank you for helping me to see what has been hidden in the past. Amen.

STEP EIGHT

Made a List

Made a list of all persons we had harmed, and became willing to make amends to them all.
—Step Eight of the Twelve Steps

You learn to salve the wounds of others by knowing and remembering how much it hurts to hurt.
—Richard Rohr, *Breathing Under Water*

An article appeared in our diocesan newspaper featuring a tribute to the life of the father of one of my son's friends. I texted my son to tell him about the article and to let him know that I would save it for him. He was glad that I'd seen it and asked that I keep it in a safe place.

Days later, when he came for a visit, I handed him the folded newspaper and said, "Don't forget your article."

"I don't want that," he said.

"What? You told me that you wanted me to save it for you," I said.

"Oh." He stopped himself, glancing down at the article I held in front of him. "I thought it was something else," he said.

"What did you think it was?" I asked.

"I thought it was an article on alcoholism."

I didn't think much about it at the time, but later that night our exchange kept nagging me. Why did it keep calling for my attention? What was I supposed to learn?

I kept wondering why he would think that I would try to advise him on his alcoholism. Then, a "share" from a twelve-step meeting that I attended the week before came to mind. A newcomer discussed all of the things her son had been doing that troubled her, and a few of us who consider ourselves to be "old-timers" were trying to encourage her to shift her focus off of her son and onto herself.

She listened to us and said, "You know, my son says that all I do is stare at him. I didn't think that I did, but maybe I do."

And we do. In the beginning of our recovery, we have a keen, all-consuming focus on our loved ones. My son's response to my handing him an article reminded me how much my past actions still affected him that day. My focus used to be right where this mom's was. I forwarded him daily devotions, articles on recovery, retreats for alcoholics, and many other things related to issues he was dealing with that were simply none of my business.

With the distance of years and growth in both twelve-step work and my relationship to God, I can see that I put a lot of pressure on my addicted loved ones. My son's reaction to the article I saved confirmed that my unrelenting focus on him left an indelible mark.

How Our Actions Affect Others

I never fully understood how much my actions affected others until I began to slow down and work these steps. Even when I prepared for the Sacrament of Reconciliation with the Examination of Conscience, I did so focusing primarily on myself. What I needed to consider, and what Step Eight asks us to think about, is how our actions affect others. Because this is a family disease, I needed to pay attention to what showed up in the ripple effects of my actions. Patterns from generations past needed to be looked at and changed. As I began this process, the truth in Numbers 14:18 became clear:

> The Lord is slow to anger,
>   and abounding in steadfast love,
>   forgiving iniquity and transgression,
>   but by no means clearing the guilty,
>   visiting the iniquity of the parents
>   upon the children
>   to the third and fourth generation.

The responsibility for our actions falls to each of us. If we hope to break the cycle of dysfunction, it is up to each of us to do it. We must take time and examine what we're doing and why we are doing it. We have to stay close to God in prayer so that he will reveal to us what we need to see. In an article comparing the Twelve Steps to Ignatian spirituality, Father Ed Dowling, SJ, writes, "There are two liabilities when we commit a sin: one, *reatus culpae*, the guilt of sin; the other, *reatus poenae*, the obligation of restitution." Father Ed felt that the sixth and seventh steps cover the guilt of sin, and the eighth and ninth steps cover the restitution. My friend, Father Peter Gautsch, OP, goes further by explaining that with both mortal and venial sin, the problem at the heart of our offenses is that they weaken or destroy our relationship with God. The idea of penance is to begin the process of restoring that relationship.

It's important for me to look at what my actions do to others as well. Program friends might tell me to "be sure to keep my side of the street clean." That is the only control that I have. While I look at my part, I must keep in mind the balance that we talked about in chapter 7. I need to remember that I am not less than human because of the actions that I've taken in the past. I am not defined by my worst sin.

I also need to steer clear of blame or justification. These actions only serve to make me look better in a moment where I'm uncomfortable seeing myself as I truly am. My greatest accomplishments don't define me either. I must be able to look at myself objectively. I am made of a combination of good and not-so-good. I have to remain cognizant of the fact that I am human. Perhaps I could try to look at myself as Jesus would.

Let's recall the scene in John 8:3–11. Jesus was in the temple area, and the scribes and Pharisees brought an adulteress to him. While the intention of these men was to test Jesus, there is a lot that we can learn from the way he proceeded.

The men told Jesus that the woman was being charged with adultery. They knew that the punishment prescribed for that crime was death by stoning; yet, they asked Jesus what they should do. Instead of casting judgment, as they expected, Jesus bent down to the ground and began writing in the dirt with his finger. (St. Augustine believed that our Lord was making a list of the sins of the men who encircled that woman. I like that theory, because it seems to go along with his next action.) The men continued to ask Jesus for a judgment, when he stood and said, "Let anyone among you who is without sin be the first to throw a stone at her" (8:7).

In the same way, as hurt as many of us have been by the effects of this disease, we must look for our part in it. If you've been around the rooms long enough, a loving sponsor will often stop your complaining by asking, "What's your part?" You see, relationships, by their very definition, are about how two or more people relate to or deal with each other. We must look for the places where we might be at fault, where we might have contributed to the problem.

If our goal is to heal, then judgment becomes irrelevant. If Jesus took the side of mercy over judgment with the adulteress, why can't we offer the same mercy to ourselves and others? It is time for us to get to work learning as much as we can about our own sinful nature. The harm caused by the addicted person is often easier to identify: bills not paid, damage to homes and cars, jobs lost, marriages ended, poor health . . . the list could go on and on. Still, we must address our fault in any of it in order to heal. We get ourselves into trouble when we start comparing our sins with someone else's. Our only job is to clear our own interior clutter.

St. Ignatius would call these character defects disordered attachments. These might be habits that our subconscious thinks will protect us but often do the opposite. If our actions don't meet the litmus test of praising, reverencing, and serving God, then they are of no use to us or our loved ones.

We can begin by looking at our life as an investigator would. What things cause me to stumble? What should I learn to avoid? What patterns do I see? What can I learn from those patterns?

It is painful for me to even think about looking closely at the ways that I've harmed others. Often, I didn't realize that what I was doing was harmful. At times I repeated what my parents did, thinking that it had to be the right way. There were other times when I knew what I was doing and that it was flat-out wrong.

For me, Step Eight is the most difficult one to face. This step requires great vulnerability. I must be courageous enough to own up to the worst parts of myself. This is a step that I have approached and walked away from many times. It can feel overwhelming.

Step Eight says: "Made a list of all persons that we have harmed, and became willing to make amends to them all."

Start with a List

I am not alone in my feelings. AA's founders Bill W. and Dr. Bob Smith (a fellow alcoholic and surgeon from Akron, Ohio) must have sensed the difficulty of approaching Step Eight because they broke it into tiny doses. We start out by simply making a list. Now, I am a list maker. I like making lists. It helps me feel as if I've actually begun the process of the work that lies in front of me.

Psychologists have found that making lists helps to establish order when things feel chaotic. It gives us structure and a plan, and once the task is completed, it can be marked off our list, giving us a sense of accomplishment. There is also the "Zeigarnik effect," named for the Russian psychologist Bluma Zeigarnik. She discovered that the brain is obsessed with pressing tasks. In other words, if we know that there is something we need to do, our brains will keep mulling it over. It will not forget. We will carry those thoughts with us, and they won't quit calling for our attention until we deal with them. Once we complete a task, the brain tends to let it go.

Along the same lines, a couple of professors, E. J. Masicampo and Roy F. Baumeister, at Wake Forest University, discovered that even though we haven't completed a task, writing it down makes us feel as if we have a plan, and our anxiety levels drop. We don't have to face the daunting notion of making amends yet (that's Step Nine). For now, we just have to start with a list. Start by just putting one foot in front of the other. "Just do the next right thing," program friends will say.

This reminds me of something that I learned one day at my husband's veterinary clinic. It was a moment when I realized that God really is in every single detail, and if we pay attention, there is always a lesson to learn.

During springtime the clinic gets very busy. One day I stopped in and asked the receptionist if my husband was still working with an animal. She looked into the exam room and said, "No, he just finished with the last horse."

I walked back and found him in the lab looking through the microscope. "What are you doing?" I asked.

"I just finished inseminating that mare and am checking the sperm's viability," he said. (Since the semen is shipped from all over the country, it is important to see how well it survived the journey.) "Do you want to look?"

"Sure." I took my place on the stool and adjusted the lenses until I could see all of those little "swimmers" moving around.

"What percentage do you think he has?" my husband asked.

"I'd guess fifty percent," I said. "What is your guess?"

"About thirty percent."

"What? It looks like at least half are alive," I observed.

"Well, that may be true, but the important number is of those sperm that are 'progressively moving forward' (PFM). That's how we score the sample," he added.

What a unique distinction. I couldn't get this insight out of my mind. We can be alive, just swimming in circles, but unless we are *progressively moving forward*, we are not heading towards new life. We are merely existing. When I am facing a difficult task, I remember that example, and I put one foot in front of the other and start with the first small task. Many people will begin this step by pulling out their Step Four inventory. By looking at my character defects, I will often remember those people who have received the blunt end of those defects. Then, I make a list of their names.

How Healing Occurs

It's always good to start the list with our family members. It's a simple fact and the subject of many a popular song that we hurt the ones we love. Have my reactions towards them been hostile? Have I made sure that they see and feel my anger and resentments? Have I taken my frustration out on them? Learning from our past actions can help us change our behavior. That is what this step is all about.

We need to change the course of our family communications. We must offer each other a chance to talk through our concerns by stating facts and leaving the accusations or defensiveness out of the equation. If we fight fair, we will hear what the other person needs, hears, or feels. Father Fred Harkins, SJ, who recovered at Guest House in Michigan, said that a visiting physician from Canada told him, "Recovery begins when the patient takes over." I see the truth in his statement. In the past, I have reacted to my life. Now that I'm taking time to examine myself and my actions, I am taking responsibility for my life. That is a response.

The next phase of Step Eight is that I need to become willing to make those amends. Again, the program resembles God's offering of free will. Nothing is forced. But if I want emotional sobriety—if I choose it—I have to be willing to attain it. Otherwise, these defects will never allow me to have personal freedom.

I can take baby steps with this aspect as well. Many in the program suggest that you make three columns. There is a column for those with whom we are willing to make amends, a column for those with whom we might want to make amends, and a column for those with whom we will never make amends. With time and practice in forgiving others and making amends, many of these names will shift to other columns. The steps will not be finished in one day, one week, or one year. These steps require a lifetime of work. Remember, if we make consistent, progressive forward motion, we are always moving towards new life.

I am learning that the amends I offer to others help me heal as well. As I began to focus on the importance of restitution for me, the offender, it brought to mind the work of a friend in my writing group. Alissa Ackerman, Ph.D., a professor of criminal justice at California State University, Fullerton, specializes in the study of sexual violence. Her focus is on understanding and preventing sexual misconduct of every kind. She gave a Ted Talk on the subject of *connection*.

"I'd really like to give you a hug, if that's ok," she said, as she opened her talk. Alissa was telling the story of what a sexual offender, who had spent the last twenty years in prison, asked of her during her participation in a restorative justice session.

Alissa not only works with sex crime survivors: she is one. Her motivation to make a difference in this problem that plagues our culture is organically born. It's hard to imagine that she would agree to the request of a hug, but she did. She has received criticism for her humane treatment of this man and others like him.

Restorative justice looks at the harm caused rather than a statute that has been violated. No further conviction is sought. Instead, each person hopes to restore some part of her- or himself that has been lost due to the trauma. The offender must listen to what the survivor went through. He must accept responsibility for the harm that was done as a result of his actions. The survivor gets a chance to be heard. She becomes more than just an object used by her perpetrator. Being heard and seen allows her to take back her humanity.

In her restorative justice session, Alissa shared that she is still afraid of the dark. She hasn't gone swimming in the ocean in seventeen years. She is afraid of human touch. Her list of fears continued to illustrate the effects of her offender's actions. Listening to her speak of the fear that she still feels almost two decades later helps the one man in the session with her begin to understand the full impact of his actions. Sitting in the circle with her, he begins to accept responsibility. This leads to healing and empathy. He then asks for her permission to give her a hug.

Let me be clear about the point that I am trying to make here: I'm not suggesting that we should compare our situations to those of people who have suffered from sexual crimes. I am not implying that they have a part in what happened to them. They do not. What I am saying is that we can learn something about healing from these sessions. Clear communications from both sides, the willingness to hear the pain of the other, and working to take responsibility for our actions can help each of us reconnect.

Gabor Maté, M.D., a Canadian addiction specialist, spoke about trauma at a "Beyond Addiction" workshop in Vancouver in 2015. He said that trauma is not the event that happened. It's not the rape or the abandonment. "The trauma is that, as a result of that, I lost the connection to myself. Hence, I lost the connection to my essential qualities: my joy, my vitality, my clarity, my wisdom, my power, my strength, my courage. That's the trauma!" He goes on to say that while the event can never be erased, the trauma can be healed. The brokenness can be repaired. With connection, healing happens.

There is no better example to prove this case than comparing Peter and Judas. Peter denied Christ three times. Judas betrayed Jesus by turning him over to the people who would kill him for a few silver coins. Each man broke trust in his relationship with Jesus.

The difference lies in the way that each man dealt with the harm that he caused Jesus. Peter faced his problems. He was sorry and remorseful. Later, Jesus asked three times, "Simon, do you love me more than these?" Peter affirmed his love for Jesus each time. He had the opportunity to amend for each of his denials and reconnect with Jesus. Judas, on the other hand, felt despair. He did not have the hope that his sins could be forgiven. His regret felt too big for God's mercy. He threw the money that he received for betraying Christ into the temple and hanged himself.

How many times have we thought that our sin is too big? How long have we carried our shortcomings with us—day in and day out? This step is the key to beginning the process of repair and restoration. It is when we can reconnect with God and others that healing occurs. Step Eight begins the process that leads to personal freedom.

WORK THE STEP

Begin by finding a quiet, comfortable spot where you can acknowledge God's presence.

- Read and meditate on Psalm 51.
- The easiest way to begin Step Eight is to make a list with four columns.
    - The first column is titled, "Person Harmed"
    - the second, "Relationship to Me"
    - the third, "Harmful Act"
    - and the last column, "Reason for the Amends"

- As you fill in the columns, reflect on these questions:
    - Column one: do you see a pattern in the people you list?
    - Column two: what are some specific ways in which those relationships have been harmed?
    - Column three: how might you think to act differently in the future? Again, do you see any patterns forming?
    - Column four: what specific harms have your actions caused others? Why do you need to make amends to the people on this list?

- Read Jeremiah 17:14. Notice the author's trust in God's healing power.

End this time of personal encounter with God by praying the prayer below or one of your own.

Heavenly Father, help me to be open to healing the hurts of the past. Give me the strength to confront the parts of myself that I am least proud of. Give me the insight to understand the harm that is a result of my actions, so that I may learn to love more like you in the future. Thank you for your love and mercy. Amen.

STEP NINE

Making Amends

*Made direct amends to such people wherever possible, except when
to do so would injure them or others.*
—Step Nine of the Twelve Steps

*For those who love, nothing is too difficult, especially when it is
done for the love of our Lord Jesus Christ.*
—St. Ignatius of Loyola

My daughter finished her final coursework for graduate school just a few days shy of Christmas. She started the long drive home the morning of my husband's office Christmas party. She arrived late that night to a house full of people, with all of her belongings wedged into every nook and cranny of her car, leaving only enough space for the dog. As she got out of the car, her facial expression gave her away. She was tired, pale, and lost.

For the first time in her twenty-six years, there was no more school in front of her. She'd left her boyfriend and cohort friends and mentors four hundred miles behind. Until now, there had always been a plan. Her life had been prescribed for her. Now she would have to chart her own path. Because she was so rattled, I doubt she knew how grateful I was to have this time with her. You see, between her brother and father's disease and her sister's health problems (my youngest daughter had a chronic condition that also affected us), I felt like I'd given her the shaft while she was growing up. In fact, I knew that when things were really rough, I left her to fend for herself more than a person her age normally would have had to do. She was responsible. *She can handle it*, I thought.

I knew that my actions could be chalked up to our difficult situation. However, that did not negate the fact that I saddled a teenager with more responsibility than she was equipped to handle. I also knew that our situation didn't take away her hurt feelings. I can only imagine the fear, insecurity, and neglect she must have felt. This time that we would have together would give me the opportunity to try and make up for some of the damage I had caused. For a long time, it felt like I'd blown it with my kids. I'd grieved the fact that I didn't slow down and do things differently while they were younger. That had been the subject of many counseling appointments and prayers. This new chance gave me a glimpse into the depths of God's generosity.

Over the next few months, I made it a point to listen and be present with her. I made her dinners, did her laundry, and watched television with her. We went on walks. We were able to connect in a way that we couldn't have previously, when the disease of addiction had entered our lives.

Then one day, after five months had gone by, she came bounding down the stairs to tell me that she'd gotten an internship in Texas. I was happy and excited for her. I knew this meant that she was probably moving away, but it all seemed okay now. It felt as if I had righted some wrongs.

When we have committed an offense against another person, whether intentional, careless, or accidental, the action taken sits between the two of us. It takes up space in our relationship, keeping us at a distance. The proverbial elephant in the room makes it impossible for intimacy to happen or develop. Until it is acknowledged and dealt with, it will always be there, and the relationship remains stagnant.

My son's sponsor once spoke at my twelve-step meeting. One point that he made about making amends has stayed with me. He once told his sponsor that the statute of limitations had run out on some of his offenses. He would not need to worry about making amends for them. His wise mentor told him that there is no statute of limitations on our guilt. It will always remember. And so, it is important for our mental and spiritual health to deal with everything.

The morning my daughter left, my heart felt full; it was an equal mix of gratitude and grace that filled me up. As we stood in the garage, marveling at how she'd fit so many of her things into such a small space once again, I savored this moment. The months we'd spent together had primed our relationship for me to make an apology that she would be able to receive.

I told her that I recognized how hard her teenage years must have been and that I didn't intend to neglect her. I didn't mean to leave her alone to fend for herself, not because I didn't love her or because I didn't want to spend time with her. I did it because at the time, I didn't know what else to do. I continued, "I know you were hurt by all of that. And what hurts you, hurts me. I want you to know how sorry I am and how blessed I feel that I was able to have this time with you." We hugged each other tight, and she drove away.

I went into my quiet house and cried tears of relief. The chance to make amends can seem scary, but it is worth the effort when we set out to rebuild relationships. It feels good to try and fix what we've broken.

Step Nine says, "Made direct amends to such people wherever possible, except when to do so would injure them or others."

Making Amends

Steps Eight and Nine cast our gaze outward. How have my actions affected others? If I am to model Christ, what kind of job am I doing?

What actions should I take to clean up the messes I've created? To understand this step, we need to look at the meaning of the word *amends*. Is an amends merely an apology? The answer is no. While an apology is part of an amends, it is not enough. The dictionary says that *amends* is "a reparation or compensation for loss or damage or injury of any kind."

Making amends also includes a change in behavior or a new way of life. Your apology and reparation will be meaningless if you continue behaving the same way that you have in the past. The ultimate goal in making amends is the *restoration of relationship*. In the book *Falling Upward*, Richard Rohr helps us see that not only do we need to seek forgiveness from those whom we have hurt, but we also need to forgive ourselves. This will result in mending our relationship with ourselves and others as we saw in chapter 8 when we looked at restorative justice. Rohr writes, "If you have forgiven yourself for being imperfect and falling, you can now do it for just about everybody else. If you have not done it for yourself, I am afraid you will likely pass your sadness, absurdity, judgment and futility to others."

Better relationships will hinge on making sure that we are trustworthy to people we have hurt in the past. The action I took with my daughter was an effort at making direct amends. I looked at all the ways in which I'd fallen short with her in our relationship. I tried to look at the effect my behavior might have had on her. I tried to imagine being a teenager with parents who were absent and in chaos. She must have felt frightened and alone. I tried doing for her what I hadn't done when things went off the rails. I focused on giving her quality time, and then I apologized. And even now, I'm making sure that our relationship stays a priority.

Sometimes, it is impossible to make direct amends. This might be the case when someone is still too angry with you to allow you to see him or her. It may be that it's too painful for that person to revisit the past. In these instances, *indirect amends* can be made. Simple actions like offering prayers for them will be appropriate. Changing your behavior, also refered to as *living amends*, would be a good option. Or you could volunteer as a means of reparation. When I first started my program of recovery and realized that I could not fix my son, I had an overwhelming need to do something. I realized that my attempts at keeping him safe were probably the things that harmed him the most. These would fall into the "what you fear, you create" category. I needed to try and repair some of the damage that I'd caused.

While raising him, my priorities were askew. This was not because of him; it was because of all the fear I carried. My son was just as God intended, full of unique God-given gifts. But I had an expectation that he needed to do certain things to be all right. It was an unconscious, irrational rubric passed from one generation to the next.

As I worked Step Nine, I felt the need to make a lot of changes in order to be the kind of mother that God wanted me to be. In the beginning, I thought that I needed to busy my hands. Maybe that would keep my mind on my own business, which is what twelve-steppers kept steering me to do. As I mentioned back in chapter two, my program friend Annie was taking a twelve-step meeting into the jail, and she invited me to join her. I'd never been in a jail before, so I was a bit nervous. But there was a gnawing feeling that I should go and serve in a way that stretched me beyond my comfort zone. So, I decided to at least give it a try.

Our first meeting was held at the end of a hallway that had been partitioned off because there was no meeting room. About ten women were present. They were polite and friendly. Once the meeting was over, we gathered together in the center of our space and formed a circle to pray the Lord's Prayer. Instinctively, I clasped the hands of the two women on each side of me as we did in my home group. The girl to my left tugged her hand away and let out a little yelp. I looked down and saw that her hand was swollen to about twice its normal size.

"Oh my, I'm so sorry," I said, resting my hand against my leg.

"It's okay," she said, offering her arm. "You can hold on above my hand."

When I looked into her eyes, I realized that she wasn't just saying that to be polite: she wanted human touch. I realized how isolated these women were from their families. This experience opened my eyes to one of the devastating effects of confinement. At that moment I vowed to go back. I knew that I could not help my son directly, but I could be present for someone else's daughter. For the next five years, I went once every week, and some semesters twice a week, to volunteer at the county jail.

I learned that over 80 percent of the inmates in our county jail had a drug- or alcohol-related charge. Over time, I began to see the disease from the perspective of the addict or alcoholic. I saw firsthand how this disease affects every sector of the population and the impact that it has on my community. I started to learn how much these young women did not want to have their disease. I saw them struggle with the way that their actions affected their families. I got a good, up-close look at the shame. I stopped seeing inmates and saw mothers and daughters instead.

My indirect amends to my son became a gift to me. It connected me with a section of the population with which I had never associated. I noticed that most of my happiest days were those that I spent in the county jail. I knew that this all had to be in God's plan. He always seemed to do things in a way I never would have imagined.

There are many ways that indirect amends can be carried out. If you pray about it, an idea will always come to mind. One of my favorite "making amends" stories is that of Venerable Matt Talbot. He is known as the patron of alcoholics and addicts. Matt Talbot grew up in Dublin, Ireland, shortly after the Irish potato famine. He was born into a large family with an alcoholic father. He took a job delivering Guinness to pubs at the age of twelve. He did this to try and help support his family, since his father's wages were used to buy alcohol. Sadly, he began to drink the dregs of alcohol from the empty bottles that he returned to the brewery.

His drinking progressed. By the age of thirteen, he too was an alcoholic. Soon, his wage couldn't cover the amount of alcohol that he consumed. At first, he borrowed from friends and ran tabs at the pub. Then he began to steal. He even stole a violin from a blind street performer. By age twenty-eight, he decided that he'd had enough. He quit drinking, "taking the pledge" for sobriety, which was organized by the Capuchin Franciscans and others in the Catholic Church. At first, he pledged not to drink for three months. And he kept extending his pledge. He replaced drinking with prayer, daily Mass, fasting, and service. By the time he died, he had remained sober for forty-one years.

In early sobriety, he worked hard and used his wages to pay off his debts, help his mother, and fill the needs of the poor. When it came to the violin that he stole, he could not get the blind street performer out of his mind. He searched for him for seven years. Unable to find the violinist, Matt donated the amount of money that would have covered the cost of a new violin to a priest and asked him to pray for that man's soul daily.

Amends Are for Me, Too

We need to make amends. Sometimes it's hard to admit it to ourselves because it's a frightening thing to do. As I went through this process, I realized how much I needed this step for myself as well as the person to whom I was making amends. We are made for each other.

Making amends is key to reconnecting with those whom we have hurt. It is that loss of connection that hurts us the most. Sister Maria Edwards, RSM, a Sister of Mercy, RCIA director, and licensed counselor at my church, told a story that illustrated the importance of our need to stay connected to our loved ones. Sister Maria was teaching a class of eighth-grade students, and as the class came to a close, she gave a homework assignment. She told her students that she wanted them to be sure to hug their family members and tell them that they loved them.

The next time she saw a young man from that class, he thanked her for the assignment. When his father was leaving for work the next morning, he hugged him and told him that he loved him, just as Sister had asked. There is no way he could have known that, as his father went to work that morning, he would be killed in an automobile accident. The boy said that he would always be grateful that those were his last words to his father. Even though the boy and his father had no grievances between them, it was important for the boy that, when his father left this earth, their connection to one another was intact.

The Scriptures record a story in John 21:15–19 that shows us the importance of connection. Before Jesus' Crucifixion, Peter had denied Christ three times. Later, the risen Christ talks with him: "Jesus said to Simon Peter, 'Simon, son of John, do you love me more than these?' He said to him, 'Yes, Lord; you know that I love you.' Jesus said to him, 'Feed my lambs.'" Two more times Jesus asks the question, "Do you love me?" Twice more, Peter affirms his love for Christ. Then he is given a task—"Feed my sheep."

Does Jesus need to hear Peter say that he loves him? Peter even says, "Lord, you know everything; you know that I love you." No, Jesus didn't ask this question for himself. He asked for Peter's sake. He gave Peter a directive, three times, one for each of the denials. Jesus helped Peter mend their relationship. He gave us an example of how to do that.

As humans, we tend to muddy the water on making amends. There is no way to remove a mark that we have left on others. The best that we can do is to make an effort to repair what we can and resolve to live differently going forward. After Jesus asks Peter for the third time and Peter responds, Jesus then says, "Follow me."

I've worked these Twelve Steps a few times. As I look at how they are set up, I see that in Steps One through Three, order between God and me is restored. He is God, and I'm not. I have to let him be God if this is to work. That is how I repair relationship between me and God.

Then, I get busy cleaning myself up. Steps Four through Seven break that work into tiny pieces that I can do one step at a time. It's hard work, but every single bit is necessary. Those steps help me repair my relationship with myself. Steps Eight and Nine help me repair relationships between me and others. The sole purpose of that work is to allow God, who is love, to flow through me to those I love. This step work removes all the things that might block that flow.

There are times when it's hard for me to see God through my humanity, and so I see him through the lens of my earthly father. We are sitting in our recliners and my dad fixes his eyes on mine, holding them steady so that I can hear what he has to say. He's pointing a finger towards me while holding his cigarette. The ashes are so long that I can't imagine how they haven't fallen to the floor. And then he says, "I gave you one job." The sound of disappointment that I continue to hear is still a part of the healing that I need to work towards.

When I feel the weight of my offenses, that is what I hear in my mind—*you had one job*. I only had to love them. With the benefit of hindsight, that is easy for me to see now. But at the time, there was so much that I didn't know. The gift of these steps and Ignatian

Spirituality is that we get the opportunity to learn about proper relationships. We learn how to stay close to God and use the example of Jesus to teach us how to live and love.

Perhaps Jesus is putting the question to us, "Do you love me?" Or maybe the question should be, "Do you know *how* to love me?" For the answer to this question, we can return to the book *The Return of the Prodigal Son*. I like the way Nouwen looks at this story from the perspectives of the father, the brother, and the son—he is looking at the *relationships*. How should we love others in relationship? How do we maintain connection?

In the past, when I read Steps Four through Nine, I thought that they were all about judging who I am and the job that I'm doing as a human being. Now, I see that these steps are preparing me to receive love and hold it within, so that it might have the opportunity to heal me. Then I might be able to offer it to others. How beautiful is that?

Step Nine allows us to put the love that we proclaim into action. Do we want to be defined by our mistakes or to live despite our mistakes? We can affirm our love for Jesus and our loved ones when we accept our mistakes and do the work needed to repair and reconnect with both God and others. Then we will have accepted Jesus' call to "follow [him]."

WORK THE STEP

Begin by finding a quiet, comfortable spot where you can acknowledge God's presence.

- Read and meditate on Psalm 65.
- Begin by making a list of amends that you need to make. Organize this list into three columns:
  - one listing for those that will definitely be made
  - a second for those that might be made
  - and a third for those that will never be made

- Then, review your list and decide how you will make amends.
  - Choose which amends can be made directly.
  - Choose which amends will be made indirectly.
  - Choose how you will make living amends.

- Read Luke 23:33–34. Notice that even in his agony, Christ's love for us abounds.

End this time of personal encounter with God by praying the prayer below or one of your own.

Heavenly Father, help me forgive those who have hurt me. Since I seek mercy for my offenses towards others, please help mend my relationships. Show me how to love those whom I've offended in such a way that it heals the hurts that I may have caused. Thank you for your kindness and love. Amen.

STEP TEN

Continued to Take Personal Inventory

Continued to take personal inventory and when we were wrong promptly admitted it.
—Step Ten of the Twelve Steps

When the devil wants to attack anyone, he first of all looks to see on what side his defenses are weakest or in the worst order; then he moves up his artillery to make a breach at that spot.
—St. Ignatius of Loyola

I stood outside of the classroom near the sergeant's desk, waiting for the lawyer and his client to leave my Homeward Bound room. I was irritated that they would use our space. We had a lot of work to do and only a small amount of time to cover it. My students were not allowed to congregate in the hallway, so I waited for the lawyer to finish before I asked the correctional officers to call my students in. We were careful to follow the rules. It was important to show respect to these women. I wanted to be on time and give them their full hour of class. I fully believe that when we show respect, we receive it.

As I stood there waiting, I heard the unmistakable noise of inmates making their way from the courtroom. If you are in a jail for any length of time, you become familiar with the sound of the slow-gaited, shackled, and cuffed inmates. I looked up and saw them coming single file towards me. As they rounded the corner, I recognized one of the women in the line. My first impulse was delight. I hadn't seen her in years. But before that second had even elapsed, it felt as if hope and joy were being sapped from my very being. The minute that our eyes met, her head dropped. It made me feel sick to see her feel that way.

"Michelle, how are you?" I asked.

"I've been better, Mrs. Jean," she said, as she disappeared behind the heavy doors leading to the pods.

Michelle had been one of my students in the first year I volunteered. She was silent for the first half of the semester. She carried so much shame that it took a long time for her to speak up. Over time, she began to reveal a little more of herself. By the end, she routinely asked to close our time with prayer. She was one of the women whom I thought would surely make it. And now, here she was again, back in jail.

I remember silently praying, "What am I doing here, Lord? Am I a fool to think that I could help anyone? Or am I here only for my pride?" My head was spinning.

The lawyer and his client left. My students joined me, but I was distracted during our entire hour. I knew that I had to chase down those feelings. Why did I feel as if a wet blanket had been draped over me? What was really going on?

For most of my life, whenever my feelings caused me pain, I responded in a couple of ways. My personal favorite was running away. If I felt uncomfortable, I fled. My thinking was that if I could outrun the feeling, I wouldn't have to deal with it.

My second coping mechanism was stuffing. I would refuse to look at my feelings. Instead I pushed them deep down inside, busying myself with all sorts of things. I often tried minding the business of others. Sometimes I would try to make myself feel better by eating sweets. Or I might just binge-watch something on television or go shopping. If those feelings continued to crop up, I'd find another way to distract myself.

Over time, I realized that the use of drugs and alcohol did the same thing for my loved ones that my running and stuffing did for me: They helped to avoid dealing with feelings. Isn't that an interesting state of affairs? We really aren't all that different. I was surprised to learn that if you boil it down, people don't use or drink to have fun. They use and drink to feel different. They are uncomfortable with the way that they feel, so they use a substance to change that feeling or make it feel different.

That day at the jail, I went to my car, sat in the parking lot, and asked God to help me figure out why I felt so bad. Did I feel bad for Michelle or did I feel bad for myself? As I sat there in the quiet of my car looking out over the large brick building, adorned with twisted barbed wire along the perimeter of the roof, I realized that the incident in the hallway was another version of what I had done with my addicted loved ones. I was upset that my work there didn't fix Michelle. I was still wrestling with Step One after all these years. I still wanted to be the god of my understanding, except I wasn't aware of that until things didn't go my way. It wasn't until I was able to slow things down that I could even look at the unpleasant feelings that washed over me that afternoon. The time that I sat with my emotions allowed me to trace them to their source. Then, I was able to see what I had been doing.

I felt upset for Michelle, too. I hated seeing her live out the consequences of her actions. It is never easy to watch someone you care about continue to hurt her- or himself. Those feelings hit a little too close to home. They triggered early memories of my loved ones finding and then losing their sobriety. The highs and lows take an awful toll on your ability hold out hope. I realized that by choosing to work with others who suffer from this disease, I would be opening myself up to the hurt that comes along with it. Walking away from that work in the jail would have been so easy. It made sense to leave this disease behind and never look back. Working with people who have addictions is hard. You often see them fail over and over again. You see them get hurt. It is very difficult to watch.

But I needed to remember the positives, too. While working with these women, I gained new perspectives that took me out of my own self-centeredness. I felt needed there. And if I am perfectly honest, I needed them, too.

Self-Examination

My work with the Twelve Steps was beginning to pay off. Before, I would have carried the discomfort with me, refusing to look it in the eye. I would have taken those feelings and transferred them to others around me. With the help of my program, I could now look for the roots of my problems and pull them up from their source.

Steps Four and Five help us to identify and confess our moral inventories to God, ourselves, and another trusted person. Steps Six and Seven help us remember that we can't do it alone. We need God's help to remove our defects of character. Steps Eight and Nine ask us to look at how we've affected others. They set out to reconnect relationships that have been separated by self-centered actions. Since these steps have brought us to a healthy place in relationship with God and ourselves, Step Ten helps us maintain order. It asks us to take inventory each day and to address our problems as we see them.

Steps Four through Ten focus on making various inventories, all of which have something to do with helping us understand what it is that we *feel*. I was beginning to see how this process incorporated God, my true self, and others into my daily life. Time spent with my sponsor and home group helped me see that these inventories were not intended to point out my flaws for the purpose of judgment.

Instead, they gave me an awareness of how I respond to the emotions that come up. What were my defense mechanisms and how were they working in my life?

I've been told by friends in the program, and by counselors, that our feelings are not right or wrong, they just are. They are a part of the unique creation that is "me" and that is "you." Perhaps they are a system of communication between us and our Creator. I began to see that feelings are not there to cause us pain but to help guide us.

This idea is illustrated in a poem that I've heard many times in recovery circles. It was written by Mewlana Jalaluddin Rumi, a theologian and Sufi mystic born in 1207, and translated into English by Coleman Barks.

The Guest House

This being human is a guest house.
Every morning a new arrival.

A joy, a depression, a meanness,
Some momentary awareness comes
as an unexpected visitor.

Welcome and entertain them all!
Even if they are a crowd of sorrows,
who violently sweep your house
empty of its furniture,
still, treat each guest honorably.
He may be clearing you out
for some new delight.

The dark thought, the shame, the malice,
Meet them at the door laughing
and invite them in.

> Be grateful for whatever comes,
> because each has been sent
> as a guide from beyond.

There are those who feel that once we've reached Step Ten, we've come to the maintenance portion of the program. But have we? Is all the heavy lifting truly behind us, or are we now asked to take all that we've learned in the steps and apply it to our lives each day?

Step Ten asks me to review my actions, today. What has happened within the confines of the last twenty-four hours? Is there something I've done that needs to be corrected? Can I set out to make amends now so that it doesn't take emotional energy away from me and those I've offended?

Step Ten says, "Continued to take personal inventory and when we were wrong promptly admitted it."

Consciousness

The Alcoholics Anonymous slogan, "One day at a time," reminds us that we need to stay present today. If we worry about the past, we can easily fall into depression, and if we think too much about the future, we can easily become anxious. Today is the only time that I can influence.

Step Ten helps us remember to stay vigilant. If we faithfully practice this step, we will learn to listen to ourselves as if we were a silent observer. We will learn to be aware of why we are doing what we are doing. In *Breathing Under Water*, Richard Rohr writes that if he were to recommend a way to best approach the tenth step, he would encourage us to do an examination of our personal consciousness. Because this step is a personal inventory, we are called to pay attention, not judge. Being conscious means that we are focused on being aware of and responding to our surroundings; it is being awake.

This practice of vigilance reminds me of the time Christ spent with his disciples in the Garden of Gethsemane, just before he was taken into custody. As Jesus awaited his arrest and subsequent crucifixion, he asked his disciples to wait with him and stay awake, keeping guard. He didn't ask for this once or twice but three times. And every time, the disciples failed him by falling asleep.

How about us? Are we staying present with Christ in the midst of our day? Do we truly realize that we are never alone? At an Ignatian retreat, I was told that the word *alone* means "all one," and when we are alone, we can best experience the presence of God. When we bring an awareness of God into our consciousness, we bring safety. The notion that our Creator is present with his creation gives us a sense of being enough. If we can sit with that knowledge and accept it as true, we might feel safe shedding the skin of our false selves.

In *Breathing Under Water*, Father Rohr makes a point for finding what is good about ourselves in true consciousness: "Whenever we do anything stupid, cruel, evil or destructive to ourselves or others, we are at that moment unconscious, and unconscious of our identity. If we were fully conscious, we would never do it. Loving people are all highly conscious people."

We need to learn to recognize the purpose and meaning of everything we do. Can we stop the automatic reactions and offer a response instead? How are we able to achieve that goal?

Detachment is a big part of recovery. We are asked to detach with love from the insanity of the disease. A detached person is a nonaddicted person. Can we also detach from who we think we are, to be enlightened as to whom God is creating us to be? Father Rohr goes on to say, "For properly detached persons, deeper consciousness comes rather naturally. They discover their own soul—which is their deepest self—and yet have access to a Larger Knowing beyond themselves."

If I sit with the idea that I have enslaved myself to an image that I've created of who I should be for the purpose of being enough or being protected, then I realize that what is true and real and created by God is far better than anything I could ever construct.

For me, Step Ten is a step for daily growth. It helps me maintain my position with God and see myself for who I am and *whose* I am. It helps me be who I am called to be for others. It can seem very complicated and a big task to boot. St. Ignatius of Loyola had a great knack for looking at complicated ideas and creating practical tools to help us apply them to our everyday lives. In his Spiritual Exercises, you can find a reflective prayer practice that accomplishes all that Step Ten asks us to do.

Created about five hundred years ago, the Examen prayer, just as the Twelve Steps are, is based in our whole-life experience. It also recognizes that we only live in the present moment and can only be effective at managing one day's worth of existence at a time.

During a day, we might be carrying shame from the past or fear of the future. Constantly looking back and straining to look ahead busies our mind, takes up space where our awareness could be, and makes us absent from the realities of our day. Without knowing it, we bring these same burdens into the next day. Unless we are able to connect our feelings to our experiences, deal with them appropriately, and then let them go, we will remain out of touch with our spirituality. Ignatius's simple prayer helps us do all those things.

The Examen

There are as many variations of the Examen prayer as there are people who pray it. I use a version that feels right for me and seems to fit into the rhythm of my evening routine. It consists of five simple steps: Presence, Gratitude, Review, Sorrow, and Grace.

The first step, *Presence*, asks me to remember that I am in the presence of God. I take a few moments to remind myself that I am not alone. I sit with his loving presence as I hope to review my day. Then I ask him for help. I ask to see what I need to see.

The second step is *Gratitude*. Gratitude is an important part of the recovery process. Whether you are the one with the addiction or you are the family member of someone who is, gratitude is a powerful tool of recovery. One of the first things that I was asked to do when I began my twelve-step program was to create a gratitude list. Many times, when someone comes into this program, his or her mind is consumed with all of the problems. Over time, the problems are all you can think about. My twelve-step friends call this "living on the hamster wheel." A gratitude list forces you to stop staring at the problems. When you train yourself to see the gifts that are given to you, you are able to see that your life has balance. Your focus has shifted. The problems are still there, but the gifts are too. When you choose to focus on the good, hope reminds you that anything is possible.

The third step is *Review*. Now that I recognize that God is with me, and I am aware of and thankful for the many gifts he imparts to me each day, I can look with peace on yesterday. I then review my actions throughout this day. I look back on every exchange with others. Which actions keep calling for my attention? I try to recall my feelings during each exchange. I wonder what my motivations were. When did I feel as if all was right with the world? When did I feel alive—even if the circumstances around me weren't ideal? Ignatius referred to these times as moments of "consolation" or nearness to God.

Next, I review the parts of my day when I might have felt a nagging feeling of foreboding. Was there general uneasiness about something that looked attractive on the surface? Did I feel despair? These moments Ignatius called "desolation" or feeling distant from God.

The fourth step is *Sorrow*. Once I've reviewed the actions for which I feel sorrow and remorse, then I ask God for his forgiveness. I ask for his help in future encounters. And I give thanks for the times that I have felt consoled—aligned with his will.

The final step is *Grace*. Now I ask for the grace to learn from my mistakes and to prepare me for the day ahead. As I drift off to sleep, I have ended my day by reviewing it and preparing for the next, with God as my guide.

The beautiful thing about Step Ten and the Examen prayer is that they build an everyday relationship with God. Each day I get to know him a little better. I am paying attention when he leaves little gifts for me to discover. It confirms how much he really loves me. And when I fall short, I witness his mercy and grace. I start to see that these are further expressions of his love. I come to realize that his will is always the wisest choice. And because I've witnessed his love firsthand, my need for control is lessened.

WORK THE STEP

Begin by finding a quiet, comfortable spot where you can acknowledge God's presence.

- Read and meditate on Psalm 73.
- Begin Step Ten by keeping track of the good. Start a daily gratitude list on paper so that you can see how much you've been given.
- What behaviors and attitudes have you noticed that you were unaware of before?
- What feelings did you notice that may have resulted from regrets from the past?
- What feelings did you notice that come from fear of the future?
- How did it feel to make amends as soon as you caught yourself hurting another?
- Read 2 Timothy 1:7. Notice how God provides for us.

End this time of personal encounter with God by praying the prayer below or one of your own.

Heavenly Father, thank you for this day. Help me remember to check in with you each day so that I may notice and appreciate the good and deal with the not-so-good. Show me the things that you want me to see. Give me understanding. Help me to be ready to live today and prepare for tomorrow. Amen.

STEP ELEVEN

Prayer and Meditation

Sought through prayer and meditation to improve our conscious contact with God as we understood Him, praying only for knowledge of His will for us and the power to carry that out.
—Step Eleven of the Twelve Steps

To give and not count the cost, to fight and not to heed the wounds, to toil and not to seek for rest, to labor and not to ask for reward, save that of knowing that I do your holy will.
—attributed to St. Ignatius of Loyola

Each morning during the warmer months, I wake up, slip on my house shoes, pour a cup of coffee, and head out to the back porch. My dogs pace between the coffeepot and the back door. The dachshund, Lucy, stands at my feet while I fill my cup, whispering a whine to nudge me to move faster. Louis, the standard poodle, stretches out in downward dog and yawns as he keeps an eye on my next movement. Their communications are clear.

Outside, my husband waits. Since the day that we married, he has always gotten up before me. "Good morning. How did you sleep?" he asks. I report the status of my sleep and ask him the same question. After the pleasantries are out of the way, we grow quiet. For about thirty minutes, we respect each other's time alone in the peace that accompanies daybreak.

We keep up this ritual because there is something magical that happens each morning as the light breaks through the darkness. The birds announce the sun's arrival before we see it coming. They start out with quiet song, but as the sun makes its way over the horizon their chorus picks up volume. It's as if they are the only creatures that understand how lucky we are to have this new day.

The whip-poor-will's song ushers me back to a time when I was young, sitting on the porch with my dad. We'd hear the katydids introduce themselves to us, as well as some birds. My dad would call back to each bird, and we'd wait to hear them respond. Later, we'd hear the "caw-caw" of the crows. My heart still yearns for the sounds of childhood and home. Only, now I know that home is not a place but a destination that we each travel towards. There are moments when I feel a nearness to God and those cravings are satisfied.

I guess we come out here each morning seeking what is *holy*. Innately, we know the importance of starting our day here in the still of morning. Perhaps we seek because there is a constant unfulfilled yearning that calls for us to seek. I stumble as I try to put words to this search. But if I see it, it is familiar.

One day as I was scrolling through Instagram, I heard a song playing by a band that I'd never listened to before. The song drew me in. It felt like recognition. I wanted to understand its lyrics. I googled it and found a YouTube video in which the North Carolina folk-rock band The Avett Brothers told the story behind their single, "Every Morning Song." The chorus is what captured my attention. The lyrics point to our need to interpret what hope will look like, or in the case of this song, sound like, for each of us individually. So, although we can know there is hope for each of us, we have to discover the melody of that morning song for ourselves.

Since mornings are when I connect with God, I stopped and listened to the song. In the video, one of the brothers talks about an aunt who suffered from cancer. In her last days, she told him that she had to do this (dying) on her own. She said that nobody could do it for her. She just hated that she couldn't help those around her deal with the reality of the situation.

I'm starting to see that my relationship with God—my higher power—is something that I must develop alone. I can tell you about how good he has been to me, but you must see that for yourself in your own life. I can tell you how and where I find him, but you will need to look for him where you feel his pull and presence. I can even tell you what grand feelings I get when I feel him close, but my words aren't enough to illustrate his presence in your life.

Step Eleven starts with the word *sought*. Right off the bat, I know that the first order of business is that I need to look for God. Saint Ignatius is best known for encouraging his fellow Jesuits to go out and look for God in all things. Through his relationship with God, Ignatius learned that God is active in our everyday world. This can be illustrated by the words of the Jesuit poet and priest Pierre Teilhard de Chardin, who writes, "God is not remote from us. He is at the point of my pen, my pick, my paintbrush, my needle—and my heart and my thoughts." We need to seek God because that search is a reminder that we can't live without the guidance of a power that is greater than we are. Each step is a gentle reminder of this truth.

The next words of Step Eleven give us the means by which we are able to look for God—*through prayer and meditation*. I am not a theologian, of course, so I can only share with you my own experience, strength, and hope. When I think about sharing my feelings on prayer and meditation, I realize that a lot has changed about my beliefs and my practice related to these things.

Prayer and Meditation

I think that I can best communicate my experience with prayer in the same way that many AA members speak about their recovery at open speaker meetings. In those meetings, an AA member prepares a talk that answers three main questions.

1. What was it like? (experience)
2. What happened? (strength)
3. What am I like now? (hope)

Each speaker is given roughly forty-five minutes. In AA, the first question "What was it like?" is sometimes referred to as the "drunka-logue," where the person describes the *experience* of active addiction.

The second portion of the talk answers the question "What happened?" The person describes a defining moment when he or she reached a decision that something needed to be different. Some will call it a bottom. My son calls it a jumping-off point. Or maybe he or she encountered God, and a shift occurred that changed the whole trajectory of his or her life. This section of the talk illuminates the *strength* that they found within themselves to make a change.

The last portion of the talk answers the third question "What am I like now?" This last bit of the speech illustrates the growth experienced by the speaker, which offers *hope* to those who are there to listen.

The *Catechism of the Catholic Church* helps us understand what true prayer is:

> "Prayer is the raising of one's mind and heart to God." . . . But when we pray, do we speak from the height of our pride and will, or "out of the depths" of a humble and contrite heart? He who humbles himself will be exalted; *humility* is the foundation of prayer. Only when we humbly acknowledge that "we do not know how to

pray as we ought" are we ready to receive freely the gift of prayer. "Man is a beggar before God." (CCC, 2559)

When I think back over my life of prayer with God, I see a superficial relationship that slowly became real and intimate. If I am perfectly cognizant of "what it was like" before, then I know that God was not at center. I was clearly trying to run the show. I wasn't sober to that reality, though; it was hidden deep enough that I would not have to acknowledge it. If you had asked me if I trusted God, I would have said "Yes." That part of me that wasn't fully awake to the reality of my life would have believed it too. But I was afraid. My actions did not live out the truth of those words. I didn't know God well enough to trust him with the direction of my life. And I didn't trust him with my son. The noise of the fear was so loud and blinding that it consumed my attention. I could not see beyond it. I couldn't even see my hand in front of my face.

Back then, I was a wandering fool. Quite unconsciously, my early prayers were carefully crafted to maintain control. It was as if I was writing a legal document where I took great care to make sure there was no loophole for God to slip through that might leave me vulnerable to his will. Other prayers were like grocery lists: "I need this and that, and I'd really like to have it by this date. Oh, and Lord, you could probably grant this wish by taking this action . . ." In other words, I told God what to do, how to do it, and by when to have it done. Surely, I was unconscious of my actions or maybe I was still in denial. Either way, that was my *experience* . . . a classic drunkalogue.

So, what happened? How did my prayer life change? Where did the strength come from? The short answer to all those questions is: *I don't know*. Perhaps it was grace. But I do remember the first honest prayer that I ever prayed. I remember it because of two things. First of all, I was scared to death to pray it. Second, I received an answer quickly, and life changed after I received it. I had this request in my mind for weeks, and one afternoon, I found my courage and whispered these words: "Please show us the problem."

My petition was the first acknowledgment that I needed help and that I was willing to receive it. Without any real awareness of it at the time or for some time to come, that simple question moved God back to center. I cried "uncle!" I knew and accepted that I couldn't figure it all out.

That prayer was a turning point. Once I uttered that truth-filled, simple prayer of petition, it was as if I had plugged myself into the ultimate energy source. I felt connection. That little prayer was the beginning of my conversion that still unfolds today.

My earlier prayers were what the writer Anne Lamott calls "beggy prayers," and they were not meaningless. They represented that initial step of raising heart and mind to something bigger than myself. There was recognition. Until I offered that fearful whisper of a prayer—with no strings attached—I had only put my trust in myself. No wonder I was still afraid. This new prayer was the first time that I let go of expectation, outcomes, and my loved ones.

During that period of my life, I only prayed. I didn't give much thought to meditation. I'm not sure that I even knew what it was. Meditation didn't find its way into my daily practice until after that first real prayer. The *Catechism of the Catholic Church* helps us with understanding what meditation is:

> Meditation is above all a quest. The mind seeks to understand the why and how of the Christian life, in order to adhere and respond to what the Lord is asking. The required attentiveness is difficult to sustain. We are usually helped by books, and Christians do not want for them: the Sacred Scriptures, particularly the Gospels, holy icons, liturgical texts of the day or season, writings of the spiritual fathers, works of spirituality, the great book of creation, and that of history—the page on which the "today" of God is written. (CCC, 2705)

Today I see prayer as the portion of my conversation with God where *I* do the talking. During meditation, I *listen*. I had finally made a request that required trust. It was a first. I had really only told God what to do in the past. Now I was desperate. I needed to know. So, I started to listen.

God showed us the problem within one or two days. There was indeed a problem in our home, and it was a big one. We couldn't tackle it alone. I was in the greatest time of need of my life, and God answered. So, I asked more questions, and I began to listen more.

That is when I began to wake up. I was conscious of the fact that God could and would be active in my everyday life, if only I would let him in. I was beginning to experience his love. While I was still afraid and unsure, I was out of options. I guess that was one of my bottom moments. That is what happened. That is how I found my *strength*, and it changed me.

What am I like now? What is my prayer life like today? Where does my hope come from? To explain that, I will need to give you a little backstory of how I learned to pray.

As a Protestant, we didn't really use written prayers other than the Lord's Prayer. Most of my prayers included the four things that can commonly be heard in any prayer: thanksgiving, petition, adoration, and intercession. I learned this format from ministers and Sunday School teachers who prayed with me during my formative years. My grandmother also prayed very vocally. In the beginning, this was the only way that I had been taught to pray.

As I was coming into full communion with the Catholic Church, I began to use other written prayers. The obvious prayer to learn as a new Catholic was the rosary. I fell in love with the words of the prayer of St. Francis. "Come Holy Spirit, fill the hearts of thy faithful . . ." is something that I keep in my pocket for times of need. An all-time favorite written prayer is from Thomas Merton's book, *Thoughts in Solitude*:

> My Lord God, I have no idea where I am going. I do not see the road ahead of me. I cannot know for certain where it will end. Nor do I really know myself, and the fact that I think that I am following your will does not mean that I am actually doing so. But I believe that the desire to please you does in fact please you. And I hope I have that desire in all that I am doing. I hope that I will never do anything apart from that desire. And I know that if I do this you will lead me by the right road, though I may know nothing about it. Therefore, will I trust you always, though I may seem to be lost and in the shadow of death. I will not fear, for you are ever with me, and you will never leave me to face my perils alone.

During our family's difficult times, written prayers would often help me convey my needs when my mind was so busied that I couldn't even recognize what they were. They gave me direction. My regular use of the Serenity Prayer began on the day of my first twelve-step meeting. These prayers helped keep me honest. They kept me from trying to manipulate God.

My preferred method of prayer today is what Ignatius called *colloquy*, or conversation with God. I remember watching my grandmother make candy when I was in college. She wasn't able to find the recipe that she was looking for, and so she said aloud, "Lord, how am I to make this candy?" A minute or two later, I heard her say, "Oh, thank you, Lord," as she scurried to write down the recipe that came back to her memory. She taught me that nothing is too small for God's attention.

There is a little book that helped me recognize what my part should be in prayer. My husband and I were going to his veterinary school reunion in Columbus, Ohio, and we stopped at a Barnes & Noble. This little book, *Help, Thanks, Wow: The Three Essential*

Prayers, written by Anne Lamott, greeted me at the front of the store. The author makes a really good case for keeping our prayers simple. She says that besides silence, she only needs those three prayers.

If you think about it, "Help" is a prayer of petition and intercession, "Thanks" is a prayer of thanksgiving, and "Wow" is a prayer of adoration. For me, those three prayers helped raise my heart and mind to God. They pushed me to trust God to handle my problems and the problems of others the way that he saw fit. They were also a catalyst that taught me to learn to detach from trying to play God.

All these prayers and ways of meditating have brought me to the place I am today. I realize that my prayer is my relationship with God. Most of the time, I don't use many words. I choose silence to keep myself ordered. And meditation is a big part of my day.

Each day my prayers and meditations look a little something like this: First thing in the morning, I ask God to help me to see and do what he would have me do; during the day, I sit and talk with God the same way that I talk to a trusted friend; at day's end, I practice the Examen prayer. It's a call and response kind of relationship. I'm learning to ask and then wait. If I don't know what to do, I do nothing, or I might go to Scripture or to a book I am reading. That is how things are now. The hope that I can offer you is the fact that my life has direction and peace, no matter what kind of things are going on in it. Fear and anxiety have no place in my relationship with God. That is my *hope*.

Step Eleven says, "Sought through prayer and meditation to improve our conscious contact with God *as we understood Him*, praying only for knowledge of His will for us and the power to carry that out."

Praying for Others

In *Breathing Under Water*, I read something that really stuck with me: "The first mind sees everything through the lens of its own private needs and hurts, angers, and memories. It is too small a lens to see truthfully or wisely or deeply. I am sure you know that most people do not see things as they *are*, they see things as *they* are."

Could it be that the steps are meant to emphasize the need to look at our lives from a broader perspective? Can we get outside of our small, day-to-day world and see God's world and our part in it?

One event happened that helped me see the power of prayer and how close God stays to those who suffer. It was many years ago, during a time when our son was in active addiction, and we, like other parents faced with this problem, were worried sick.

My husband woke me up one morning very early. In my groggy state, I was confused about what was going on. He asked me to come into the kitchen and sit at the table because he wanted to show me something. As I sat down in the chair, Matt opened his Bible in front of me. He began explaining that he was so worried about our son that he began to cry out to God, "Show me what to do to help." Then he randomly opened his Bible and put a finger on a page before looking at it.

The text he found himself pointing at was Mark 9:14–29. The heading in the Bible says, "The Healing of a Boy with a Demon." Let me start by telling you that I personally feel that the disease of addiction involves spiritual warfare, and many times we both felt that this disease is like a demon that takes over the person. When Matt randomly opened to this page and pointed at this heading, we knew that we were being guided with Scripture.

> When they came to the disciples, they saw a great crowd around them, and some scribes arguing with them. When the whole crowd saw him, they were immediately overcome with awe, and they ran

forward to greet him. He asked them, "What are you arguing about with them?" Someone from the crowd answered him, "Teacher, I brought you my son; he has a spirit that makes him unable to speak; and whenever it seizes him, it dashes him down; he foams and grinds his teeth and becomes rigid; and I asked your disciples to cast it out, but they could not do so." He answered them, "You faithless generation, how much longer must I be among you? How much longer must I put up with you? Bring him to me." And they brought the boy to him. When the spirit saw him, immediately it convulsed the boy, and he fell on the ground and rolled about, foaming at the mouth. Jesus asked the father, "How long has this been happening to him?" And he said, "From childhood. It has often cast him into the fire and into the water, to destroy him; but if you are able to do anything, have pity on us and help us." Jesus said to him, "If you are able!—All things can be done for the one who believes." Immediately the father of the child cried out, "I believe; help my unbelief!" When Jesus saw that a crowd came running together, he rebuked the unclean spirit, saying to it, "You spirit that keeps this boy from speaking and hearing, I command you, come out of him, and never enter him again!" After crying out and convulsing him terribly, it came out, and the boy was like a corpse, so that most of them said, "He is dead." But Jesus took him by the hand and lifted him up, and he was able to stand. When he had entered the house, his disciples asked him privately, "Why could we not cast it out?" He said to them, "This kind can come out only through prayer."

What did we take away from this passage? My husband learned that our prayers were essential. I agreed with him but felt that we also needed to work towards trusting God more. More than anything, it offered us hope. I began to see that when we reached out, God responded in a way that soothed our worries. He made himself present in our darkest times. Little windows into his movements in our lives became more and more visible.

One Father's Day, just before my son got sober, we all met for early Mass and then brunch. We'd arrived so early that we went to get coffee before Mass. There was a panhandler in a wheelchair out in the parking lot of the coffee shop. He asked, "Could you spare a little money for a Father's Day supper?"

My husband said, "We are going to go in for coffee first. I'll catch you on the way out."

After we got our coffee, the girls and I got into the car and my husband met up with the man in the wheelchair. It took a while for him to come back to the car. I glanced back to see that they were in conversation. When he returned to the car, I said, "It looks like you had a lot to talk about." And I noticed that his eyes were full.

"I asked him if he was clean and sober. He said that he was and that it was a blessing. I told him that I was sober, too, and that I agree—it *is* a blessing. Then I shared with him that I have a son who hasn't found sobriety yet, and I wondered if he would pray for him. He said he would." My husband gave him a little money and came back to the car. There was something about this exchange that moved him. It moved me, too. The Scripture that Mother Teresa often quoted came to mind: "Truly I tell you, just as you did it to one of the least of these who are members of my family, you did it to me" (Matthew 25:40).

It wasn't about the money. It was about seeing ourselves as human beings all helping each other find God. And if we were a part of that exchange, I know that God was close, hearing our prayers. It felt right.

The Angel of Alcoholics Anonymous

One of the heroes early in the history of the Alcoholics Anonymous program was a woman named Della Mary Gavin. The Sisters of Charity of St. Augustine would rename her Sister Mary Ignatia.

People in recovery simply called her the "Angel of Alcoholics Anonymous."

Sister Mary Ignatia worked as a nurse in an Akron, Ohio, hospital, where she met Dr. Bob—Bill W.'s partner in the formation of Alcoholics Anonymous. Early in her life, she'd suffered from some emotional problems, and while he worked at the hospital, Dr. Bob's shaking hands gave away his problems with alcohol. The pair understood each other and began to work together for alcoholics.

She was among the first people who recognized that addiction is a disease. When hospitals refused to see alcoholics and addicts, she found a way to list their diagnosis as something that was acceptable to the hospital. Then she sat vigil with the patients as they began the painful detoxification process. She gave people a chance to get sober and then connected them to others in recovery to help them once they left the hospital. Before each patient left, she sat down with him or her and gave him or her two things: a book, *The Imitation of Christ* by Thomas à Kempis, and a Sacred Heart badge. But they came with conditions.

To receive the badge, patients took a pledge that if they were going to take a drink, they would return the badge first. I read about this in an article written by Gerard E. Sherry titled "Sister Ignatia and the A.A." It is a powerful example of her reliance on prayer that I will share with you here:

> The telephone rang and Sister Ignatia answered it.
>
> "This is Bill, Sister. I'm sorry, but I'm going to have to send you back the Sacred Heart Badge. I've had a rough morning and I'm going out to get a drink."
>
> Sister Ignatia sighed, but quickly said: "Don't do it, Bill. Wait until you finish work at five. Then call me again. In the meantime, I'll pray for you. Whatever you do, don't send me back the badge. Keep it with you for strength and inspiration."

Sister Ignatia prayed hard all afternoon and, finally the call came from Bill.

"It's O.K., Sister, I never took the drink. I think I'm going to be all right now, thanks to the Sacred Heart and you." (*The Sign—National Catholic Magazine*, May 1956)

The Sacred Heart badge began a tradition that continues today. In meetings everywhere, tokens continue to be given. They are called chips. When alcoholics or addicts attend the first meeting, they can receive what is called a "desire chip," because they are making the statement that they desire to quit drinking. When they have thirty days of continued sobriety, they receive a 30-day chip. Chips are given for 60, 90, and 120 days, and again at six months and nine months. After that initial difficult year, annual medallions are given.

Besides the love and dignity that Sister Mary Ignatia offered the alcoholic, she was best known for promoting prayer as a way of healing, for both the alcoholics and their families. She once said that a spiritual remedy for a spiritual disease seemed logical. She believed that when families prayed for their loved ones, it relieved some of the helplessness that they felt. Furthermore, Sister Ignatia felt that church groups should offer prayers as well as programs to combat the growing epidemic of addiction. These were her words in 1954 to the National Council of Catholic Women in Akron, Ohio:

[O]f all the sinners [in the world] the drunkard is the one who *displays* his weakness and his deficiency for all the world to see. When prayer accomplishes a reformation to him, God therefore teaches us a lesson on the power of prayer. I usually give the patients a little talk after breakfast every morning. Sometimes I use this very theme, . . . some loved one has been praying for you or you would not be here; someone has been praying and making sacrifices for you, because grace is obtained only through prayer and sacrifice. Many of the patients come to me after my little talk, with tears in their eyes and say, "Sister, I know that my wife has been praying for me . . ."

God's Will

The final piece of Step Eleven is the real meat of it: ". . . praying only for the knowledge of His will for us and the power to carry that out." If we are to "keep it simple," as my program recommends, then we present our concerns to God and ask him to show us his will.

My program has brought me to this understanding that we need only to seek God's will. Saint Ignatius, too, asks us right from the beginning to seek God's will in the First Principle and Foundation. We need to learn to live out his plan. By now, we are starting to see how fruitful it is when we do that. Each time we take a step in faith, we learn to trust in God more. Prayer is the link that allows that trust to grow. *Twelve Steps and Twelve Traditions* has the prayer of St. Francis of Assisi as the prayer for Step Eleven. So, I'll close with it here.

> Lord, make me a channel of thy peace,
> —that where there is hatred, I may bring love—
> that where there is wrong, I may bring the spirit of
>   forgiveness—
> that where there is discord, I may bring harmony—
> that where there is error, I may bring truth—
> that where there is doubt, I may bring faith—
> that where there is despair, I may bring hope—
> that where there are shadows, I may bring light—
> that where there is sadness, I may bring joy.
>
> Lord, grant that I may seek rather to comfort than to be
>   comforted—
> to understand, than to be understood—
> to love, than to be loved.

For it is by self-forgetting that one finds.
It is by forgiving that one is forgiven.
It is by dying that one awakens to eternal life.

WORK THE STEP

Begin by finding a quiet, comfortable spot where you can acknowledge God's presence.

- Read and meditate on Psalm 86.
- List some of the ways that you seek God.
- How, when, or where do you most often "find" God?
- What are your favorite ways to pray?
- Look back at your life of prayer. Write down the ways that it has changed and grown.
- Do you recall specific instances when you were grateful that you *didn't* receive what you wished for? List the gifts you received by receiving God's will instead.
- Read Jeremiah 33:3. Notice the promises God offers.

End this time of personal encounter with God by praying the prayer below or one of your own.

Heavenly Father, I long to keep you close. Help me learn to pray in a way that helps our relationship grow into what you want it to become. Thank you for helping me find you. Amen.

STEP TWELVE

In All Our Affairs

Having had a spiritual awakening as the result of these steps, we tried to carry this message to others, and to practice these principles in all our affairs.

—Step Twelve of the Twelve Steps

Ad majorem Dei gloriam ("For the greater glory of God")

—motto of the Society of Jesus

I felt a real sense of accomplishment. It was only March 4 and I had just delivered our tax organizer to the accountant's office. This had to be a new record for us; we usually file for extensions.

As I changed lanes to get on the bypass that leads home, I spotted a woman walking up and down the concrete median by the turning lane. It is common to see people there, either selling the local homeless newspaper or carrying a cardboard sign asking for assistance. For years, I've struggled with what to do when I approach the homeless population. Early on, I wanted to control them as I did my loved ones who are affected by the disease of addiction. So, I wouldn't give money. That way, they couldn't go buy drugs or alcohol. Later, I fixed up little packages to keep in my car that consisted of a water bottle, an energy bar, a toothbrush, toothpaste, maybe hand warmers, and other such items. It was something I saw on Pinterest that seemed like a good idea.

Then one day, when my son and I were out for lunch, he gave money to someone on the street. I was digging through my purse and muttered that I hoped it was okay to give him cash when my wise son looked at me and said, "If you can't give without strings attached, it's not really a gift."

I once heard Father Greg Boyle, SJ, say something to the effect that giving to others, regardless of what they do with our gift, could be the only vestige of love that they will receive that day. It made me think of the gifts that God has given me. He doesn't give them to me to manipulate me to behave a certain way. They are free and clear, with no strings attached. I can make use of them or fritter them away. I realize that I have done both those things with the gifts that I have received. Who am I to judge what others do with the small tokens that I offer?

Back in my car, my heart sank a little as I pulled into the turning lane. I knew that I didn't have any cash. She looked at me and waved. I looked and waved back. It was a small exchange, one in which an onlooker wouldn't notice any communication at all, but one in which she was able to recognize that I couldn't help her out. Her face fell. It was only for a moment, as if the disappointment slipped out without her permission. But then her smile returned, and she continued walking past my car. I couldn't get that look of sorrow out of my mind, so I watched her through the rearview mirror as she approached the cars behind me. Two cars back, a lady lowered her window and handed out some cash. I was relieved.

It was twenty-six degrees outside that day. I thought about all the things that we say about the homeless. I realized that walking on ice-cold concrete in freezing temperatures with a bone-chilling wind was more difficult than any job that I'd ever done. My heart yearned for just a few dollars. I noticed that her clothes were too big. Her sweat-pants were probably two sizes too big for her and maybe her coat, too.

The sleeves were long enough that you could only see the tips of her fingers. *Her hands must be so cold*, I thought.

As that last thought ushered its way through my mind, I started pulling off my gloves. I rolled down my window, holding the gloves outside as she skipped back towards my car. "Oh, thank you so much. Now I don't have to tuck my hands inside this coat," she said. I was grateful that there was something I could do for her. The light changed to green and I drove off to continue the normal routine that I had planned for my day. Yet, throughout the morning, my mind kept coming back to that scene on the bypass. *Why did it move me so?* I wondered. It wasn't that big of a sacrifice on my part. I had another pair of gloves waiting for me at home. *I have a home, for heaven's sake.*

As I replayed the whole event over in my mind, I realized that it mattered because it was more than just the small gift I'd offered to someone in need. I was a player in a scene orchestrated by God. I was being used by him to reach her. And it brought me such great joy. It was as if passing the gloves from my hands to hers allowed me to touch the hem of his cloak. It stirred my heart.

Like St. Ignatius, I now take notice of my feelings. And, quite frankly, I felt high. It is a feeling that makes everything seem possible. This is that feeling that we all chase. The one that takes us to another place, away from our human limitation, and encircles us with love. When we try to catch this feeling with a substance or an action, it is a weak substitute that never satisfies. As Jesus said in John 4:13–14, "Everyone who drinks of this water will be thirsty again, but those who drink of the water that I will give them will never be thirsty. The water that I will give will become in them a spring of water gushing up to eternal life."

My program is all about realizing who and what is driving my life. The enemy has told us that we know as much as God does. That first lie haunts us still, getting us into a world of trouble. You see, we simply are not God. We don't know enough and we can't do enough. If God is not at the helm, then neither are we—we are most likely driven by fear or shame. Maybe we are driven by pride or greed. There can be a host of other things that motivate us. But unless we "let Jesus take the wheel," as they sing in a country song, there is no love. That feeling that brings us hope and joy will be gone.

The Eternal Exchange of Love

Back in my catechetical training days, Sister Mary Michael, OP, used to tell us that when she repeated something over and over again, it wasn't because she'd forgotten that she said it, it was because it was important and we should write it down. There was one entry that she repeated more than any other thing, from the *Catechism of the Catholic Church*: "But St. John goes even further when he affirms that 'God is love.' God's very being is love. By sending his only Son and the Spirit of Love in the fullness of time, God has revealed his innermost secret. God himself is an eternal exchange of love, Father, Son, and Holy Spirit, and he has destined us to share in that exchange" (CCC, 221).

When I think about the twelve-step program, I realize that it is an eternal exchange of love. It teaches me from the very beginning that I'm powerless. Then it introduces me to "The Power," as my friend in the program calls him. Once I learn how trustworthy he is, I hand over power. Then I get down to the business of cleaning up the mess that I've created. I begin to accept that I am made in the image and likeness of my Creator. I learn how to stay sound and in right relationship with him, and then I give back the knowledge offered to me throughout the years to new people in the program.

I didn't learn these things from a wise theologian. This gift of understanding came to me through a number of broken people like myself. These people were always there when I needed them, offering a hand to pull me up and out of the despair I found myself in. God still works with everyday people like Peter and Paul just as he used to. He can work with us, too. I wonder why we keep forgetting.

I know that I had missed that point. I began volunteering at the jail early in my recovery process. I didn't do it out of the goodness of my heart. I did it to keep myself busy. I needed a distraction that would help me stay out of my loved ones business. But once I started going, I was hooked. I noticed lives outside of my own. Not only did I forget about my troubles for a time, but I also was able to see the burdens of others. This work created a connection that helped me begin to wake up.

Step Twelve begins with, "Having had a spiritual awakening as a result of these steps." This statement points out how *each step* of this program has awakened me to a new thought: I'm not God. He is God. As I come to know the God of my understanding, I see that he's very good to me. He's so good, in fact, that I see that what he offers is more than I ever wanted for myself. Perhaps I should give my situation and loved ones to him. Maybe I should even allow him to determine the direction of my life. Next, I acknowledge that I'm human, imperfect. I see the flaws and come out of hiding by sharing these things with God and others. I work on ridding my life of these flaws but know that I will still need God's help with this work. This work will take a lifetime. I look at how these flaws have hurt those I love. I work on making amends to those people. I start a new practice of examining myself daily for the purpose of staying connected to God in our newly formed relationship. I use prayer and meditation for this connection.

I see these truths now. I am sober to this new reality. Now I'm ready for the final step. I have two missions now. I need to carry this message, which is what I am doing with this book. It's what I do at every twelve-step meeting that I attend. It is what I do when I sponsor another person. I also need to practice these principles in all my affairs. This is a holistic call to live my everyday life according to each of these twelve steps, all of the time. Since I am human, I will make mistakes. I won't be able to do it perfectly. But if I stay connected to a power greater than myself, I will be able to do the work that these steps require. That will help me maintain connection with others. These connections allow the eternal exchange of love to flow.

Step Twelve says, "Having had a spiritual awakening as a result of these steps, we tried to carry this message to others and practice these principles in all our affairs."

Practice These Principles in All Our Affairs

Step Twelve was key to Bill Wilson in his sobriety. He realized that in order to stay sober, he had to stand with other alcoholics while they sought their own sobriety. He knew that there was something magical that happened when one alcoholic met with another.

Father Greg Boyle understood the healing that occurs when we follow this ideal. In *Tattoos on the Heart* he says, "You stand with the least likely to succeed until success is succeeded by something more valuable: kinship. You stand with the surly, the belligerent, and the badly behaved until bad behavior is recognized for the language that it is: the vocabulary of the deeply wounded and those whose burdens are more than they can bear."

The women in our classes were usually within six months of their out-date. As they prepared to leave, if they were paroled or were put under probation, they started looking at the requirements for the conditions of their release. Those conditions might include having a job or taking certain classes through the probation office. Usually there were fees and fines associated with them. I learned that many of these women did not have any form of identification. They needed at least a Social Security card or birth certificate in order to secure a job or driver's license. In order to pay their fines, they needed money. In order to get money, they needed a job. To get a job, they needed an ID.

Housing was another issue. Many of these women had no place to go that would allow them to get on their feet. Or the options that they did have were not good ones. If they returned home, maybe there would be drugs or violence. As I talked with the administrator at the jail, she expressed her wish that we have a class, as part of the Homeward Bound program, that addressed these issues. Out of that conversation, the class called "Mercy Works" was born.

A couple of brave women joined me, and we began interviewing the women to see what their needs were. We got really good at figuring out how to get identification for someone who had none. We started gathering lists of recovery homes, treatment centers, and halfway houses for them to contact to get housing lined up before they were released. We helped them to see that they had options.

The mission of that class was to provide collaborative services such as transportation, food, clothing, case management, legal and civil assistance, twelve-step recovery, job searches and training, family services, and life skills with the hopes of reducing recidivism, reuniting families, and creating self-sufficiency with the help of local services and churches.

We began keeping files for each woman who passed through the program. The assessment of need was the first document to go in the file. From there, we brought in applications for whatever identification they needed to acquire. With time, the files began to grow from an empty folder to having a birth certificate, a Social Security card, letters from housing options, and sometimes even a résumé.

I remember the day when I realized the importance of that work. One afternoon I came into the classroom and handed each woman her file, as I usually did. They would always open them to see if paperwork had been added during the week. A young woman, whom I will call Natalie, looked through her file, closed it, and pulled it close to her chest, hugging it and smiling in a way that made me stop going over the instructions that I was giving them for the day.

"You are proud of that file, huh?" I asked.

"Mrs. Jean, you don't even understand. I didn't have anything when I came in here. I didn't even know who was listed as my father on my birth certificate until now." Her eyes became misty. "This file is proof that I am somebody," she said.

I was just there volunteering, checking another task off my list. Only now, I was being woken up. This was more than a list. Those were more than just documents. To her, we were curating proof of her existence. God was using us to help these women see themselves as his beloved children.

I kept thinking, *These women are a part of my town; they are a part of my community*. And yet, I would have never given them a passing glance if I had walked by them on the street before. After my time at the jail, I had changed. I'd seen the wounds. I would never be able to blindly walk past people in need again. The earlier steps helped me to wake up to God's presence in my life. Step Twelve is the time to wake up to our presence in God's world. What does he want us to do? How are we to bring God to others?

Ignatian spirituality has an exercise that might help you envision a way of accepting the call to help Christ realize his hope of a kingdom here on earth where all are welcomed and no one is excluded. It is a key meditation referred to as the Call of Christ the King. In this exercise, we contemplate how Christ calls men and women to follow him. Ignatius starts out by asking us to first imagine a call from an earthly leader that may have inspired us.

Thinking on this call, I do not feel the need to imagine much. I have a memory from a silent weekend retreat I recently attended where Greg Boyle, SJ, was our retreat director. He talked about how often people wanted to clone his gang rehabilitation program, Home-boy Industries. They wanted to use his model in their communities. He explained how that might not work in a place like Kansas or Wyoming but how there might be unique needs that both of those places had with which one of us might be able to help. Then Father Greg called each of us to think of the ways that we can help erase the margins in our own geographical areas.

In the Call of Christ the King, Ignatius then asks us to imagine that Jesus extends his invitation for us to help him create his kingdom here on Earth. What would we say to him? How would we feel? Would we resist? What aspirations do we have?

There again, I didn't have to imagine. I knew that I wanted to offer others what I'd learned about the Twelve Steps and Ignatian spirituality. Those two tools have radically changed my life. I wanted to offer these practices and the hope that they give to those who are afraid of the stigma of addiction. I wanted to offer them to my church. I wanted my voice to join with others and offer them to those who are alone.

Is there a gift that you have to share? Is there a need that you see in your community? I hope that you will take this exercise with you into prayer. God will lead you where you need to go.

I'll be blunt: not everyone is cut out to volunteer at the jail. But be assured, there are plenty of hurting hearts in your community. Just a few weeks back, I was at a twelve-step meeting when one of our members, whom I will call Frances, came in late, with tears streaming down her face. She sat down at the table, reached across and took a couple of tissues from the box. As the chairperson was reading the daily reflection, I could hear the woman next to her whisper, "Are you okay?"

"No, I'm not," she said, shaking her head while dabbing her tears.

When it came time for Frances to share, it was as if her voice wore the exhaustion that her heart carried. She told us that her daughter, who was in active addiction and homeless, had called her, saying that she didn't want to but she would be coming home. She didn't have any other options.

"She was talking so fast. She sounds unbalanced. I just don't know if I can take it every day," she admitted.

We all nodded and listened. We know the insanity of the disease. We know what it sounds like, looks like, and how it can suck the life out of any home. When the meeting was over, one member put an arm around Frances and said, "My daughter sounds unbalanced when she's high too. It's just the disease talking. It's not really her."

An old-timer joined in: "Frances, remember you have choices. You can say no. You can tell her that you are only willing to help with her recovery. You won't help her continue using."

Another person joined in and said, "You can always ask her what *she's* going to do about it." It seemed that every person there came up to Frances and offered support. The Christ in each person recognized the suffering Christ who lived in Frances.

"I was worried that it was wrong to not let her back in." She paused as if in thought, and then she said, "I like that—'What are *you* going to do about it?'"

We finished putting the room back together, and I watched as a little group of people huddled around Frances, walking her out to her car. She giggled a little and said, "I do have choices, don't I?" We all laughed. But it's a gift to us to watch a fellow human stand a little taller as she finds hope again. She had come in alone and crying. And she left wrapped in the love of God and her group, laughing. Our group might sound very wise. I'd like to say that we're a very astute group. But we are just people sharing what others have said to us in our moment of need. In the basements of churches everywhere, participation in the exchange of love goes on. The miracle is easy. And it's the coolest thing ever!

Answering the Call

In Alcoholics Anonymous, you might hear someone talk about "answering a twelve-step call." This is when a person suffering from an addiction reaches out for help to a person in recovery. They meet to see if the recovering person can help the alcoholic. There is a belief in the program that a person stays sober by helping others. I believe this to be true. But it isn't exclusive to AA. I think that anytime we reach out to anyone, it helps us and makes us better.

I got a text from a young woman, whom I will call Clare, asking me if I could meet individually with her before the group meeting. She told me that she felt "crazy." Since this is a feeling that all people of twelve-step meetings everywhere have had at one time or another, I agreed. I've been there. I've made those calls. Now, the time had come for me to answer them.

I met Clare almost two years ago. She showed up at our annual candlelight meeting, which is a special meeting when we share what we are grateful for as the person next to us lights our candle. It is a beautiful, symbolic meeting. When she walked through the door, she saw that each person sitting in the circle was holding a candle and thought she'd stumbled upon a séance. Luckily, she didn't run. She joined our circle and soon realized that we weren't trying to summon the dead. When we got around to her, she was even brave enough to share with us.

Clare is now an adult daughter of an alcoholic and the older of two children. She has taken on the role of adult and parent in her home. Like many of us in the room, she walked in exhausted and overwhelmed from the efforts of trying to hold it all together. She was so despairing that she came to us after a visit to the psychiatric ward of the local hospital. She has become a faithful member of our group. For over a year, she had been telling her family that her college study group met every Tuesday night at 7:00 p.m. During the summer months, she told them that she was going to Starbucks. No one in her family ever suspected. If you know how chaotic a home becomes when active alcoholism is present, you would not be surprised that no one noticed the pattern.

Her life continued on this path until a bout of violence forced her to make a decision. Clare decided to leave her family and her childhood home. She opened up to them about where she spent her Tuesday nights. Overwhelmed with all the changes, she considered dropping out of school, until another twelve-stepper propped her up and said, "Absolutely not!" Clare then went on to earn a 4.0 grade point average.

The day she called me, Clare and I met thirty minutes before our regular meeting, and it was clear that she was upset. She carried a lot of fear that she wasn't being the kind of daughter that she ought to be. This is very common in the beginning of recovery for family members of people with addictions. The enmeshment of an alcoholic home blurs the lines between each family member's role.

"Have you ever worked the steps?" I asked.

"Well, no, and that is something that I wanted to talk to you about," she said.

"The steps are important. You really need to learn about powerlessness. You can't fix your mom. You can't heal her. That is not your responsibility. It is between her and God. What you can do is get a sponsor and get to work on yourself," I said.

The tears started to pool in her eyes as she tried to communicate her fears. "I have some abandonment issues. And, I just worry . . . not that I'd be rejected . . . but that . . ."

"You are worried about being rejected," I said.

"No, that they might be too busy, and I might feel . . ." She stopped again, trying to hide her fear of being rejected.

"That is the reason that you need to ask. It's so important that we each learn to ask for help. You need to stop letting fear back you into the corner," I said.

We continued to talk about this issue until it was time for our meeting. We walked downstairs to the meeting room just as the chairperson was opening the meeting. After our usual readings, the chairperson said that our meeting would be held on the topic of "sponsorship." I've attended meetings for nine years now, and I don't ever remember a meeting being held on that topic. I was floored. Clare leaned back in her chair and stared at me in disbelief. I got chills. It was if God heard the cries of his brokenhearted child and said, "I hear your fears, now take my hand."

The writer Anne Lamott often says that God is "such a show-off." That night, I agreed. Clare asked her good friend and mentor to sponsor her. Her mentor was delighted to share this journey with her young friend. And I got to watch it all unfold. How lucky am I?

In the beginning of our journey with addiction, I knew that there was something of great value in this recovery process. I knew that what the Twelve Steps and Ignatian Spirituality were giving me had changed my life. I wanted to shout, "You will not believe how wonderful my life has become. Let me tell you about it!" I couldn't not share our experience, strength, and hope. It's like this amazing secret that folks in basement rooms of churches know about that those who only come through the front door are missing. The suffering is real, yes. But the healing will leave you feeling as if anything is possible.

My goal in this book has always been to let you know that you are not alone and to remind you that there is hope and help. Walk this paschal path with me and remember that resurrection is possible. I'll leave you with one last story that I feel illustrates how families get off course.

When I was in the second grade, my dad fulfilled a life-long dream of building an in-ground swimming pool for the family. It took a long time for the concrete to cure before we could begin filling it with water. It felt like waiting for Christmas to arrive. When the day finally came when we could fill the pool, all my brothers and sisters were there, along with a few cousins. My cousin Wayne, who is closest to my age, and I walked down to play in what would become the deepest part of the pool, as it was being filled. Neither of us could swim yet, but there were plenty of adults watching, and the water was nice and cool on that hot summer day.

The water rose inch by inch—so slowly, in fact, that I hardly noticed when it had reached my shoulders. Wayne, a kindergartener, was shorter than me, and so the water was now over his head. He panicked. His instincts taking over, he began reaching for me, pulling me down so that he could stand on me to keep his head above water. I was pushing him off so that I could keep my head above water. We were both going under.

My dad noticed the splashing and jumped in. He pulled us both up to the shallow end of the pool and promptly got the rope that separated the shallow end from the deep end and hooked it to both sides of the pool. He gave us firm instructions to stay on the shallow end from then on.

That memory seems so clear to me still. Maybe it is for me to remember how deeply the fight or flight instinct is wired within each of us. I like this story because it illustrates what I hope you will be able to take away from this book.

If your family has been affected by the disease of addiction, as so many families are, it's sometimes going to feel like the waters are rising above your family's heads. When it does, it is important to have tools in place that can help you and your family resist the urge to pull and push one another down in an effort to hold yourselves above the water. It is my wish that by reading this book you will have learned to tread water well enough, until you get the help that you need to heal.

WORK THE STEP

Begin by finding a quiet, comfortable spot where you can acknowledge God's presence.

- Read and meditate on Psalm 149.
- How would you describe your spiritual awakening?
- In what ways has God made himself recognizable to you in/through others?
- Can you recall a gift that was given to you that you were able to pass on to another?
- In what ways can you be a person for others?
- Read Mark 10:45. Notice how this verse aligns with Ignatius's call to be God for others.

End this time of personal encounter with God by praying the prayer below or one of your own.

Heavenly Father, I am so grateful for the gift of this twelve-step program of recovery. Most of all, I am grateful that it has helped me to know and love you more. I ask St. Ignatius to guide me as I look for you in my present-day world. Help me to use this day with every person that I meet for your greater glory. Amen.

Works Cited

The A.A. Grapevine, "The Little Doctor Who Loved Drunks" (May 1951).

Alcoholics Anonymous: The Big Book (New York: Alcoholics Anonymous World Services, Inc. © 1939, 1955, 1976, 2001).

Coleman Barks, *The Essential Rumi* (New York: HarperCollins Publishers, 1995).

William A. Barry, SJ, *Lenten Meditations: Growing in Friendship with God* (Chicago: Loyola Press, 2008, 2015).

Gregory Boyle, SJ, *Tattoos on the Heart: The Power of Boundless Compassion* (New York: Free Press, Div. of Simon and Schuster, Inc., 2010).

John Bradshaw, *Healing the Shame that Binds You* (Deerfield Beach, FL: Health Communications, Inc., 1988).

Brené Brown, *Daring Greatly: How the Courage to Be Vulnerable Transforms the Way We Live, Love, Parent, and Lead* (New York: Avery Press, imprint of Penguin Random House, 2012).

Catechism of the Catholic Church (Washington, D.C.: United States Catholic Conference, 1994).

Gerard E. Coggins, *The Anonymous Disciple* (Worcester, MA: Assumption Communications, 1995).

Robert Fitzgerald, *The Soul of Sponsorship: The Friendship of Fr. Ed Dowling, SJ, and Bill Wilson in Letters* (Center City, MN, Hazelden, 1995).

Fred Harkins, SJ, *Father Fred and the Twelve Steps: A Primer for Recovery* (Worcester, MA: Ambassador Books, 1996).

Michael G. Harter, SJ, Editor, *Hearts on Fire: Praying with Jesuits* (Chicago: Loyola Press, 2012).

Ernest Kurtz, *Not-God: A History of Alcoholics Anonymous* (Center City, MN, Hazelden Publishing, 1979).

Ernest Kurtz, *Shame & Guilt*, second edition (New York: iUniverse, Inc., 2007) [originally published as *Shame and Guilt: Characteristics of the Dependence Cycle* (Hazelden, 1981)].

Anne Lamott, *Help, Thanks, Wow: The Three Essential Prayers* (New York: Riverhead Books, 2012).

Lois Remembers (New York: Al-Anon Family Group Headquarters, Inc., 1979).

Thomas Merton, OCSO, *Thoughts in Solitude* (New York: Farrar, Straus, and Giroux, 1956 and 1958).

Henri J. M. Nouwen, *The Return of the Prodigal Son: A Story of Homecoming* (New York: Doubleday/Image Books, 1992).

James W. Pennebaker and John F. Evans, *Expressive Writing: Words that Heal* (Enumclaw, WA: Idyll Arbor, Inc., 2014).

Louis J. Puhl, SJ, *The Spiritual Exercises of St. Ignatius, A New Translation Based on Studies In the Language of the Autograph* (Baltimore, MD: The Newman Press, 1951).

Richard Rohr, OFM, *Breathing Under Water: Spirituality and the Twelve Steps* (Cincinnati, OH: St. Anthony Messenger Press, 2011).

Joseph A. Tetlow, SJ, *Making Choices in Christ: The Foundations of Ignatian Spirituality* (Chicago: Loyola Press, 2008).

Mark E. Thibodeaux, SJ, *God's Voice Within* (Chicago: Loyola Press, 2010).

Twelve Steps and Twelve Traditions (New York: A.A. Grapevine, Inc. and Alcoholics Anonymous Publishing [now known as Alcoholics Anonymous World Services, Inc.], 1952, 1953, 1981).

Acknowledgments

This book is a reality because of God's grace and help from many people.

A big thanks to Mary Armour, whose gentle and kind nature gave me the safety needed to learn to write.

Thank you to Christianne Squires for your friendship and support. I count you as one of my life's great teachers! This book would not be here without your guidance.

To Joe Durepos, I no longer hold a grudge that you called the first draft of my manuscript a "momoir." Kidding aside, I'll always be grateful that you listened when you didn't have to, that you steered me in just the right direction, and that you believed in the importance of this book. Thank you for fighting for it.

To the folks at Loyola Press, thank you for your willingness to add this crucial subject to your catalog of books. It is very important, and you've been so accommodating.

Thank you to Vinita Wright for reading each chapter as they came along and guiding me with such a loving hand.

A big thank you to Gaston Philipps for your care and consideration of the message I hoped to impart. You are a kindred spirit, and I'm so grateful that I got to work with you.

Thank you to my friends who allowed me to share a piece of your story. I hope to continue to be guided by the gift of your recovery.

To my five brothers and sisters, thank you for making me feel invincible. The confidence that you gave fortified me and helped me to never give up.

To my children, your lives have been the great teacher for mine. Thank you for your patience.

Thank you to my husband, who has spent a small fortune on books over our many years together and helped me to realize this dream.

About the Author

Jean Heaton is a blogger, writer, speaker, teacher, and workshop and retreat leader. Both her husband and son are in long-term recovery, and she has worked her own twelve-step program for those affected by the addictions of others. Heaton shares her experience, strength, and hope with others at www.jeanheaton.com.